7 MINUTES to FREEDOM

SIMPLE WRITING MEDITATIONS TO LIBERATE YOUR WRITING AND YOUR LIFE

NATALYA ANDROSOVA, PhD

North Spirit Publishers
Toronto, Canada

Editing by Katrina Tortorici of the polished-pages.com
Cover image by SelfPubBookCovers.com/Saphira
Book design and layout by Alexey Zghola
Author photo by Clifton Li

978-1-7774537-2-5 (Hardcover)
978-1-7774537-1-8 (Paperback)
978-1-7774537-0-1 (E-book)

writingdissertationcoach.com

To everyone who has ever

questioned their love of writing ...

May you lose the doubt and

let your soul fly

ACKNOWLEDGEMENTS

I am grateful to so many, but especially to ...

All my writing sisters, who sat and wrote with me through the years.

My husband Richard, who is always my first reader and cheerleader.

My editor Katrina, who encouraged my dream with her kind notes in the margins.

My students, who have fearlessly shared their writing.

All my teachers, who invited me to try and fail and try again until I learned to fly.

My parents, who have taught me how to love and dream.

And St. Lawrence Café, which provided my writing group with a welcoming space and strong coffee every Saturday.

TABLE OF CONTENTS

ABOUT THIS BOOK

IS THIS BOOK FOR YOU?

If you are reading this book, you are ready to get curious about yourself and your writing. By using the prompts in this book, you can gain direct access to your wisdom and intuition, discover your secrets, and find your authentic voice.

You don't have to be a writer to benefit from this book. In fact, this book will help you discover your voice and liberate your writing process. If you are a writer, this book can help you strengthen your creative muscle and deepen your relationship with yourself and your writing. It will give you newfound clarity on the habits of mind that separate you from the life you want to be living.

WHY THIS BOOK?

Each of us knows the difference between flying and feeling stuck. This book invites you to fly. Writing is a form of flying. It's a deep meditation on the meaning of your lived experience—a way of exploring your external and internal worlds. Writing is a wonderful tool for self-discovery. It invites you to access your soul and its guidance. It keeps you honest and teaches you how to grow by paying attention to each moment. What does this moment want to tell you? What questions does it contain? Where are you stuck? What can you learn there so that you can break free and fly again?

This book invites you to explore yourself by responding to simple writing invitations. It offers a hundred ways to write yourself free and fly again in your writing and your life. It contains a hundred invitations to write yourself clear, write yourself well, and write yourself home. This book will help you cultivate focus, attention, and clarity. It will help your writing become effortless and spontaneous. It will help you discover an authentic voice and an authentic life by attuning to your thoughts and feelings. It will make your relationship with yourself and your writing more true. It will show you how to experience each moment of your life more fully.

Writing is a form of meditation. It is also a form of prayer. You can write to ask, and you can write to hear the answers. You might not know the answers yet, but you have the power to ask powerful questions. And if you ask, life always answers.

Writing is not separate from life. The same beliefs that inhibit our writing inhibit our living. Writing is a great tool for seeing through these unhelpful beliefs. Gaining clarity on our beliefs makes our writing clearer, and in turn, writing adds clarity to our lives. While we're working on our writing, writing is working its magic on us. It's a win-win.

As the famous author Julia Cameron writes, "We should write because humans are spiritual beings and writing is a powerful form of prayer and meditation, connecting us both to our own insights and to a higher and deeper level of inner guidance as well. We should write because writing brings clarity and passion to the act of living."

HOW TO USE THIS BOOK

The book is divided into nineteen chapters, each one inviting you to explore your relationship with a different part of your life. I have only shared what helped me write myself out of confusion and stuckness into freedom and clarity. Writing has been both my journey and my guide.

Each chapter contains writing prompts—some light, some heavy. If you don't feel ready to face a certain topic, skip right to the next one. Use each prompt as an invitation to enter a short seven-minute writing meditation on the topic. You can also ignore the prompt completely and write about what's on your mind in that moment. Simply follow your thoughts and emotions, and they will take you where you need to go and show you what you need to see.

Chapter eighteen contains one hundred short three-minute prompts. They don't require too much depth and can be used when you only have a few minutes while travelling on a subway or waiting for a bus, or as a warm-up before a longer writing period.

In the last chapter, I include my own freewriting explorations of the topics in this book. I'm sharing my own raw unfinished writings to inspire you to write freely. Notice how imperfect my writing form is. Notice how I digress and leave the prompt behind and follow my pen and my heart wherever they take me. Feel free to do the same. Playfully. Without a concern for the form.

You can use this book in any way you like—either follow the prompts in order or open the book on a random page and start writing. You can do one prompt a day or continue with the same prompt for several days. You can skip some of the prompts and only use those that resonate with you in the moment. You can even return to the same prompt to explore it further and go deeper. My only wish is that you don't shortchange yourself by rushing through the prompts. Insights come from an in-depth exploration, so let thoughts and feelings percolate for a while. Give them a home in your body and mind.

This book is not about the prompts, and the next one doesn't have the power to bring you freedom. But your response might. So instead of jumping to the next prompt, stay with the one at hand. Listen to your heart. As another famous writer Bonni Goldberg said, "Writing, like any spiritual undertaking, has many paths, but only one direction—deeper".

LAST WISHES

I have a few last wishes as you embark on your journey towards yourself. Writing often becomes a place for self-judgment and perfectionism, but it doesn't have to be. Writing is a form of flying. Honour your own way of flying. Don't judge what you have written. I hope you use this book to spread your wings and fly.

Try writing with the attitude of playfulness and self-care. Be curious and courageous. Be accepting of your words and your thoughts. Be honest. It is for your eyes only. Don't worry about writing correctly. Step boldly into the fire of self-inquiry and get ready for some powerful insights. Be spontaneous and fresh, and don't rush. It's all there to be discovered and revealed in due time. What you force won't be true, but what you discover might change your life. As an experiment, trust your hand to reveal what your head might not know.

WHY WRITE?

This is love: to fly toward a secret sky, to
cause a hundred veils to fall each moment.

— RUMI

Why write? Why express anything when silence is already perfect? Why fly towards a secret sky? The truth is I don't really know. Perhaps to reveal another shade of silence, another note, another breath. To cause the veils of untruth to fall.

Writing is like a fountain. The heart doesn't ask where the fountain gets its water—it opens to the flood of writing coming in. Writing is like air. I breathe it in so I can go on living. Have to take another breath, write another line, forgive the line before for coming out awkward, silly, or incomplete. Writing teaches forgiveness, compassion, humility, and acceptance. Nothing needs to be perfect. It already is, in all its imperfection.

I fell in love with writing as a form of revelation, a tool for honesty and self-disclosure. Whatever is hiding beneath the surface can be seen. There is no power in the little me to cause the veils to fall, but writing, on the other hand, is a mystical force that reveals its power to those who can appreciate it. I have written almost daily for thirty-three years and found that the more I understand myself, the more authentic my voice is. Writing has been my prayer. It has been my teacher, and I forever remain its apprentice. I hope you, too, never stop exploring your heart.

CHAPTER 1

RELATIONSHIP
WITH YOURSELF

WRITING YOURSELF WHOLE

I want you to be everything that's you, deep
at the center of your being.

– CONFUCIUS

Writing is an alchemical process that turns pieces into wholeness. Whenever I feel like my life is falling apart, writing becomes my sanctuary. It is my sacred place to hide and rest. A place to centre and feel whole again. In this space, everything slowly returns to its natural rhythm so I can return to stillness and fullness. The writing process allows me to keep my attention on the present moment and stay with my thoughts and feelings.

When we think we are not enough and need anything or anyone to fulfill us, we suffer. When we believe that other people or things promise us wholeness, we suffer. Writing can teach us that we are not lacking anything or anyone. It can teach us freedom, honesty, and compassion, clarity and perseverance, trust and openness. It can teach us wholeness.

All that is required is to trust the process, and most importantly, to start.

Write about what you need in order to feel whole right now. You don't have to be realistic. You are not writing a plan. You are writing to find out what's true for your heart in this moment. It's a safe discovery journey, and no action is needed. Of course, you can, and probably will, act on what you learn, but for now, the focus is on the discovery itself. What do you feel is missing in your life? Who or what do you believe would make you feel whole? You can start with, "In order for me to feel whole right now, I need ..." and continue for seven minutes. No stopping. The rules are simple: don't stop, reread, or rewrite for seven minutes.

WELCOMING ALL PARTS OF YOURSELF

You are all things. Denying, rejecting, judging or hiding from any aspect of your total being creates pain and results in a lack of wholeness.

– JOY PAGE

To be well, we need to be whole. We can push away parts of ourselves and pretend they're not there, but not forever. Each day, we neglect unwanted thoughts and feelings. They are our beloved children asking for our attention, but we push them away and tell them they're unwelcome here. We deny them entrance into our world. We shut the door into their face and hope they go away and never return. If you have tried this, you know that it is futile. Eventually, when we crack the door open, all the feelings we once tried to avoid are still there—and now, there's a big angry crowd on our porch that we are forced to face.

Writing is your chance to open the door and give shelter to these unwanted thoughts and feelings one by one as they appear on your doorstep. You can give them space and attention in your writing. You can hear them out. It might be hard to do so, but in the long run, you have a chance to welcome back all parts of yourself that you have lost touch with in the course of your life journey. This is your chance to integrate them and feel complete again.

Right now, take seven minutes to reflect on a part of yourself that you have been pushing away for a while. It can be an old pain, emotion, thought, or part of your body that you have neglected recently. Today, open the door and invite it in. Ask it to speak to you and promise to listen without talking back. Simply write down what it has to say. You can begin with, "Dear ..., I'm sorry I have been pushing you away. I would like to hear you out. Please tell me anything you want to express ..." and write down the response without judging it.

RECONNECTING
WITH HONESTY

There is only one journey. Going inside
yourself.
– RAINER MARIA RILKE

Writing doesn't allow us to fool ourselves for too long, and if you are anything like me, you've tried to do it. Writing allows us to meet ourselves in the present moment, exactly as we are—with compassion for being human and flawed. No shaming our imperfections, and no judging the parts of ourselves that we're afraid to meet. Just self-compassion and curiosity, appreciation and flow.

Writing keeps us honest. It doesn't matter whether we're wearing a new mask or the one we've worn for years or decades. The mask drops when the pen touches the paper, even if it takes a couple of pages to come back to ourselves. There's a silent wisdom that has our best interests at heart

26

and comes pouring forth through our writing, even when our mind doesn't want to accept it. We know this wisdom by feeling lighter because lying to ourselves is heavy. The trick to discovering it is not knowing before you write things down.

Each of us has some secret dreams and aspirations that we have never shared with others and might even be afraid to admit to ourselves. What is secretly tugging at your heart strings at this moment? What would you love to explore? You don't have to quit your job and change your life path just yet. For now, just explore a secret interest of yours, especially if you've kept it a secret from yourself. The following sentences are here to help you make your discoveries. Finish them as quickly and honestly as possible without planning your answers in advance:

If I weren't afraid to fail, I'd …

If I weren't afraid to embarrass myself, I'd …

If I were more confident, I'd …

If I could start my life over, I'd …

If it didn't seem so crazy, I'd …

If I weren't afraid to try it, I'd …

If I didn't have to worry about money, I'd …

If I were honest with myself, I'd admit that …

If I knew for sure that I would be successful, I'd …

Even though I am good at my job, what I'd really love to do is …

If my life were extended by a hundred years, I'd explore ...

If I could design a perfect job for myself, it would be ...

If I look deeply at the way I spend time each day, I notice that ...

Take seven minutes to reflect on anything that surprised you in your responses.

WRITING TO DISCOVER
YOUR SELF-ESTEEM

Self-esteem is the reputation we acquire with
ourselves.

– NATHANIEL BRANDEN

Self-esteem is such a mysterious concept. No one knows for sure where it comes from. In fact, most of the time, we are not even aware of it. We only notice it when we are surprised by our own reaction to someone's comment. That's when we realize how important it is, and how many decisions and actions it informs, even when we are oblivious to it. Especially when we are oblivious.

Since it has so much power in your life, it might be worth spending some time investigating it. You can reclaim some of the power you gave away by exploring your self-esteem and bringing your unconscious thoughts and ideas into awareness by freewriting about it.

Start your exploration by freewriting in response to the following questions. Take as long as you need, and feel free to stay with any question longer than with others:

What is my understanding of self-esteem?

Where did I learn to see myself the way I do?

What are my sources of self-esteem now?

What makes me feel better about myself these days? Who does? Why?

What are some ways I seek external validation?

What am I most ashamed of? Why? What does it say about me?

What are some of my strengths that I am proud of?

What are three things I have accomplished that I am most proud of?

What are three goals that I am working towards that make me feel happy?

Freewrite about one answer that resonated the most for seven minutes.

PLAYING AN ARCHAEOLOGIST

Be as you wish to seem.

– SOCRATES

Before we can meet our true self, we often have to dig through layers of self-definitions. By self-definition, I mean the many stories and beliefs about who we are. The trouble is we define ourselves without noticing. We only notice our stories when we get triggered. But then it's too late, and we find ourselves spiraling down the black hole of reaction. For example, if someone criticizes our decision, we can immediately jump into defending: "I'm not stupid! I'm not weak! I'm not going to be insulted like this!", etc.

There are many ways to define ourselves—by our age, role in society, job, gender, appearance, success, ability to speak well, you name it. Our beliefs about ourselves can get in the way of freedom. Freedom to not react. Freedom to not have to defend our self-image. Writing is a perfect archaeological site to dig out all our beliefs one by one. By playing an archaeologist, you can gather quite a collection of jewels—the ones that limit us to the need to react. If you dig them out now, next time you might recognize them and stop before the reaction happens.

What do you get insulted by? Try to remember some of your most common defence statements. For example, if you often say, "Don't talk to me like this!", ask yourself, "Like what? Like you have no respect for me? Like I'm not important?" Keep digging until you find the jewel — the underlying self-defining belief that feels attacked. In this case, "I deserve respect" or "He doesn't respect me". Keep digging for meaning by exploring what triggered you. And what that said about you. What self-image did it threaten? The self-image of being smart? Young? Cool? Strong? Right? Capable? Important? An expert?

Based on your most common self-defence statements, make a short list of how you see yourself. The statements don't have to be true. Just something that reveals your self-image. For example:

I am smart

I am a great communicator

I am helpful

I am kind

I am beautiful

I am …

Were you surprised by anything on your list? Freewrite about it for seven minutes.

MEETING YOUR INNER CRITIC

*The first and greatest victory is to conquer
yourself; to be conquered by yourself is of all
things most shameful and vile.*

– PLATO

If you have never met your inner critic, consider yourself lucky. Most writers know this annoying presence all too well. They usually come unannounced, especially when we are attempting something challenging or creative, like writing. They often use negative comments to interrupt the creative process and to take away our confidence. They can even paralyze our creativity. The funny thing is when it comes to their commentary, they have a very limited repertoire of remarks and seem to say the same thing to each of us. Let's compare notes, shall we? Here are some things my inner critic says when I write. Do any of these sound familiar to you?

You don't know what you're talking about.

This is stupid.

No one is going to like what you have to say.

You're going to embarrass yourself.

You will never get it right.

You will never get it done on time.

This is not good enough.

You will mess it up again.

You can't write.

What are some things that your inner critic says to you? Make a list of their comments and suggestions. Don't rush— let them speak, so next time they show up, you can welcome them by saying, "I've been expecting you" and go right back to your writing. After finishing the list, freewrite about any insights that came from meeting your inner critic face to face.

TALKING WITH A MIRROR

The face is the mirror of the mind, and eyes
without speaking confess the secrets of the
heart.

– ST. JEROME

Mirrors can be so truthful that, at times, they become unbearable to look into. They reflect without judgment, but we are not always ready to see what they have to show us. It's hard to see what we know to be true and to notice things we wish we hadn't. Not just in our appearance, but in our eyes. Those are the hardest to deal with. We love seeing love and hope in our eyes but hate seeing sadness and despair. Do you remember the day when your relationship with the mirror became complex? The day you stopped seeing beauty and began to focus on imperfections? Today, writing will give us a chance to investigate all of this.

First, an easy prompt. Reflect on your relationship with a mirror and write down anything that you can remember about its evolution. When did it start? When did you first notice something in the mirror that you didn't like? Has it changed since? Is there something that you have always loved about your reflection? Start with, "My relationship with the mirror has been ..." and freewrite for seven minutes.

Now that you looked at the evolution of your relationship with the mirror, use this fun exercise to look at your present relationship with it. Imagine that you were a mirror reflecting your own image. Pretend you are looking at yourself from the point of view of the mirror. Describe in writing what you see. What does this person (you) look like? What do they seem to know? What have they been through? What are they hiding? You can start with, "This person seems ..." and write about anything that you have noticed for the first time.

DEEPENING THE RELATIONSHIP WITH YOUR SELF

Poetry may make us from time to time a little more aware of the deeper, unnamed feelings which form the substratum of our being, to which we rarely penetrate; for our lives are mostly a constant evasion of ourselves.

– T. S. ELIOT

Staying on the surface of things seems safe because the boundaries are well defined and protected, and we feel in control. On the other hand, going deeper into our feelings or beliefs, into our dreams and fears may be painful. In fact, it may feel like cutting. We are moving from the surface down to the core and opening ourselves to the truth. We are breaching the boundary between the inside and the outside. We are leaving the safe and solid surface and going down to the unprotected vulnerable core.

What will you find there, at the very core of your being? Do you even dare look? You might be afraid to uncover darkness that you are not ready to meet, so you are doing your best to never go there and avoid it instead. It may seem like a safer choice, but you run the risk of never meeting your deeper self, deeper dreams, deeper truth, or deeper fulfillment. Don't make this mistake.

In what area of your life are you treading water? Where are you avoiding meeting your own depth? Where do you not trust yourself to discover the deeper truth? Is it in your relationship with someone else or in your relationship with yourself that you resist delving deeper? What hidden wisdom of yours do you reject? Do you leave solutions to your health and wellbeing to experts when you know in your heart where the problem is? Where do you intuit more than you are willing to admit? You can start with, "Even though I don't usually admit it, I know deep inside that …" and freewrite for seven minutes about anything that comes to mind.

CHAPTER 2

RELATIONSHIP
WITH OTHERS

FINDING CLOSURE IN ALL RELATIONSHIPS

Beginning today, treat everyone you meet as
if they were going to be dead by midnight.
Extend to them all the care, kindness and
understanding you can muster, and do it with
no thought of any reward. Your life will never
be the same again.

– OG MANDINO

Relationships are messy. Period. If you are anything like me, you have experienced those relationships that end abruptly in a storm of misunderstanding, and before you have a chance to process anything or find closure, it's already over. You didn't get the fairy tale ending you'd imagined. You didn't even get a chance to understand what transpired or ask why. It happened so fast, and there was no time to sweep things clean. You still want to say something, explain yourself, be heard. But it's too late.

Writing can help you find closure. Right now, you have a chance to clean up every unfinished relationship that still bleeds energy from you. It can be a relationship with a parent, child, partner, or even a relationship with an unfinished project or an unfulfilled dream. You can hand it over to the divine power of life by writing a symbolic prayer for the relationship. In this prayer, you can express anything you need to express so that you can let go of the pain you've been carrying and find peace and compassion for yourself and the other.

Write a prayer for the relationship itself, for yourself, and the person involved, as well as for everyone else who is going through a similar situation. If you don't like the word "prayer", you can call it a letter to life, God, or the universe. Write anything that you need to express. Ask anything you didn't get to ask, and say what you wish you had said in the moment. Write whatever comes to mind until you feel empty, full, exhausted, and at peace. Write until you feel that it's done. Continue until you feel the release of energy and can sense a new space inside and a new freedom. It might be best to tackle one relationship at a time, but you can use this exercise whenever an unfinished relationship is draining you of vital energy. You can start with, "Dear life, I wish my relationship with … ended differently. I wish we could … I wish I could …, etc."

FEELING SAFE WITH ANOTHER

A true friend encourages us, comforts us,
supports us like a big easy chair, offering us
a safe refuge from the world.

– H. JACKSON BROWN, JR.

Each of us wants to feel safe. We want to feel safe in the external world, but most importantly, in the internal world of our mind. Where does the feeling of safety come from? Often, circumstances have nothing to do with it. Even in a safe environment, you might be playing self-made horror movies on the screen of your mind, making yourself feel scared and unsafe. Or you might be lost in the middle of a rainforest, feeling completely safe with a person you love and enjoying the exhilaration of the adventure instead of registering the real danger of the situation.

Does feeling safe have to do with people you are with? You know from experience that not everyone in your circle of family and friends makes you feel safe. You wouldn't share your secrets or your pain with all of them. You know intuitively and clearly who can be trusted with your secrets and who can't. What exactly makes you feel safe around some of them and not around others?

Remember a moment when you were with someone who made you feel safe. Write about that moment with that person. The person need not even be alive to make you feel safe. You can simply invoke their spirit and tune into the feelings it inspires. What did you feel when you were in their presence, or when you spoke with them?

Write down in detail everything you remember about the moment when you felt safe around this person. What was it exactly that made you feel safe in that moment—the look in their eyes, or the way they listened and gave you their uninterrupted attention? Was it their compassion, enthusiasm, support, or encouragement that made you feel safe to open up? You can begin with, "I remember feeling completely safe with …" and go on for seven minutes.

WRITING THROUGH
A RELATIONSHIP CHALLENGE

*Every relationship that we have in our
lives—our contact with each person, place,
and event—serves a very special, if yet to be
realized purpose: They are mirrors that can
serve to show us things about ourselves that
can be realized in no other way.*

– GUY FINLEY

Relationships are hard. There's no way around it. Sooner or
later, a relationship goes through a crisis, and each of us
must learn some difficult lessons. That's what relationships are
for—to teach us something we didn't know about ourselves. Of
course, you can always run away from the challenge and leave
the relationship behind. Chances are you will run into the same
lesson in the next relationship.

Writing can help you learn the lesson right where you
are, without leaving yet another relationship. It can help you

44

work through the challenge with compassion, humility, and understanding. As an experiment, just this one time, don't analyze the complexity of the situation. Psychology is very useful, and there are plenty of professionals who can help you uncover the unresolved childhood traumas and the resulting defence mechanisms. The way of writing is different. Let me share with you how to write through the heart of any relationship challenge.

Think of a challenging situation in your current or past relationship. Visualize the other person standing in front of you. Look at their face without thinking and observe their eyes for a while. Try to see beyond their appearance. Sense their deeper being. Now find that same sense of being inside yourself and feel the same life force inside both of you. Staying in touch with that same life force in two different bodies, write a letter to the other person's inner being, their soul, if you will. It's not important what you call it, as long as you feel connected to it and address it in your writing.

You can use the person's name to start with: e.g. "Dear John's soul …". Ask their soul anything you want to know, and don't question their response if it comes. Write a dialogue, but not between two persons—between two beings. You can request anything, but stay clear of demanding. You can express any feelings; just avoid blaming or complaining. Express how you feel about the relationship and your wishes for the future of this relationship, even if it involves dissolving it peacefully. Speak about hope for resolution and growth in both of you. Don't analyze anything. Feel instead. Discover your own meaning, not blame. Find your heart, and not your point of view. Keep looking until you're no longer at war with anyone or anything. Keep writing until you feel empty of thoughts and feelings for the moment. Write until you feel peace and compassion for both of you.

And now, from the safety of the present moment, write a compassionate letter of love and support to yourself as you are (were) going through this challenge. Express compassion and any other emotions that could help the past you to get through this challenge. Talk to your self who is (was) lost and scared and show them some love. You can begin with, "I still remember how I felt when ..." and continue for seven minutes.

WITNESSING

When you look at people, you should look at
more than what you see on the surface; you
should try to find a soul.

– VINCENT D'ONOFRIO

It seems like all of us secretly love people watching. We like becoming an unexpected witness to something sweet or beautiful, like a man dropping on his knee in front of his girlfriend in the middle of the sidewalk or a good Samaritan helping an elderly cross the street. At the same time, we are also tempted to look at something dark or dramatic occurring in front of us, like a car crash or people having a loud argument in public.

I wonder why we are drawn to witnessing others go through their dramas, their days, their lives, and their stories. I wonder why it's so attractive to sit in a cafe or a park, sipping coffee, and watch people's faces as they walk by, trying to guess their thoughts and emotions, trying to guess their life stories. What feeling does it give us? An outside perspective to the dramas of life? It's as if we get to live vicariously through others by witnessing the ups or downs of their lives and not participating. Maybe we even get to feel some feelings and emotions that we don't get to experience directly in our life. We are safe as we are watching the spontaneous unfolding of life in others. There is some secret wisdom I intuit in the act of witnessing.

In this exercise, you can people watch in your imagination. Pretend that it's a late night, and you're sitting in your room, looking outside through a large window. There's a building right across from where you're sitting. What kind of building showed up your imagination? Is it a small house or a modern high-rise, a condo, an office building, a concert hall, or a mansion? It's dark outside, but all the windows are lit, and you can see what's happening inside.

Scan all the windows and pretend that you can zoom into one of them. What drew your attention to this particular window? Write about what you noticed. What seems to be happening inside? Who is there? What are they doing? Do they look like someone you know? What do they want in this moment? What does it remind you of? What does it make you think of? Is there anything that has a meaningful connection to your life? What would be your wish for the situation you are observing? Freewrite for seven minutes.

48

LEARNING THE LESSONS

Life is an unfoldment, and the further we travel the more truth we can comprehend. To understand the things that are at our door is the best preparation for understanding those that lie beyond.

– HYPATIA

We are all blessed by teachers. They come in many shapes and often don't look like teachers, but their lessons are powerful nonetheless.

At one point or another, all of us go through pain. Pain is a great teacher, even though we usually refuse to look at it and try to forget about it as soon as possible. We numb ourselves or go into blaming mode in order to avoid feeling the intensity of pain. Writing offers a way to learn from pain and become stronger. And the best part is if you learn the lesson now, you don't have to repeat it later.

We learn some of the biggest lessons from pain because when it's unbearable, it makes us pay attention, so we can no longer avoid it and are forced to look within. As hard it is to accept, pain is one of the greatest teachers that can come into our life. When used wisely, it marks the beginning of each of our journeys from our head to our heart.

Think of a lesson you are learning right now (or had to learn recently). Start by freewriting about what happened, and how it felt at first. Consider what you are learning about yourself by going through this challenge. What inner strength do you have to draw on in order to get through this? What are you learning to appreciate more? Whom can you relate to better as a result of your experience? What did you start noticing that you had never noticed before the incident? Write about an emotional or spiritual shift if you perceive one. You can start with, "Right now I'm learning about …" and continue writing for at least seven minutes.

WRITING TO FIND COURAGE

The secret to happiness is freedom ... And the
secret to freedom is courage.

– THUCYDIDES

We all need heroes. They give us courage and faith. They can be cartoon superheroes, parents, friends, or strangers who affected us deeply within a few minutes of meeting them. We admire, respect, and revere them, but this is just half the story. The story is not really about them. The story is actually about the hero inside each and every one of us.

Your heroes bring out the best in you and teach you who you are. They embody what you wish to discover in yourself. Their actions, their struggles, their decisions can inspire you to persevere in the face of adversity and motivate you to connect to the best part of yourself, especially in moments of darkness when your faith is tested.

Think of someone you admire. What exactly do you admire about them? What have they done that is worth your respect and admiration? What have they done that you would like to do yourself? What qualities do you admire in them and would love to develop? What specific actions have they taken in the face of adversity? Freewrite about one of your heroes for seven minutes. You can begin with, "I admire ... because ..."

CHAPTER 3

RELATIONSHIP
WITH LIFE

MAPPING OUT
YOUR JOURNEY

*Do not go where the path may lead, go
instead where there is no path and leave
a trail.*

– RALPH WALDO EMERSON

Each of our life journeys is unique. Your journey has been customized with different challenges, lessons, and people you were supposed to learn from, and so has mine. How often do we take the time to think about the journey as a whole? If you are like me, it's not very often. Instead, we tend to be completely absorbed by the daily minutia and our never-ending to-do lists. Writing can help you take a good look at the big picture and find yourself on the map in order to see exactly where you are in your life in this moment.

Today, reflect on your life journey by drawing your life path as a simple map. It only has to make sense to you. Use a full page for the entire map and take twenty minutes to draw your path. Draw and write the names of important events, people, and places—those that really made a difference in your life. Nothing needs to be true to scale. All you need to do is keep drawing the hills and the valleys of your journey, the dark and the light times, the happy and the sad ones.

When you are finished with the map, freewrite about anything that occurred to you as you were drawing your life journey. Don't rush your reflection and write about anything you felt and discovered. You might also want to go back and add to the map as you write and remember certain events.

Start with where you are right now and write about where you've been and where you are going. You can begin with, "It has been quite a journey ..." and write nonstop for as long as you feel like. Find your own process and have fun exploring your life by switching between freewriting and drawing for the next hour or so.

RIDING A BICYCLE

Happiness is not a matter of intensity but of
balance, order, rhythm and harmony.

– THOMAS MERTON

In one of my writing groups, students were asked to make twenty sentences that start with "I still don't know ...". One student shared her writing, and the first thing on her list was, "I still don't know how to ride a bicycle." Afterwards, she listed nineteen other items and ended up freewriting in detail about struggling to find balance in her life. What she didn't notice was that the very first metaphor that came to her mind was riding a bicycle, which is all about finding balance.

The truth is, regardless of what we are writing about, we simply cannot write around ourselves, whether we notice it or not. That's why writing is such an effective tool for self-discovery. Riding a bicycle is a great symbol for living our lives—we all know that in order not to fall off, we must maintain a sense of balance and keep moving. We would be

56

able to move through life much more gracefully if we were always able to maintain balance. Writing can help us find it. Using metaphors can also help us gain clarity, momentum, and focus in our writing and in our life.

Think about facets of your life that you're desperately trying to balance right now. What are some things that you would like less of in your life? What are some things you would like more of? Start by drawing a vertical line in the centre of the page. Pick one of your current roles in life, whatever that role might be—a student, a wife, a mother, a father, a person in charge, an athlete, etc. On the left, list the responsibilities that stress you out the most. On the right, list everything that brings you joy and inspiration. List the aspects of your current role that you love most. After you finish both lists, freewrite about one or two items from your lists. You can start with, "What stresses me out the most is ..." or "What I love the most about being a mother (a daughter, a teacher, a freelancer, etc.) is ..." and freewrite for seven minutes. Keep writing until a new sense of balance emerges.

WRITING A DREAM LIFE

Beware the barrenness of a busy life.

– SOCRATES

Who doesn't dream of achieving great things in life? What makes them great depends on the person. Sometimes, our personal dreams clash with the socially accepted dreams, like building a house, building a career, building a family, etc. You may be dreaming of building a shelter for abandoned animals, but your family expects you to go to medical school, and so you listen to their voice of reason and abandon your own dreams or put them on the back burner.

But there comes a moment in your life when you realize that those dreams and goals are not yours, and you don't know why you are pursuing them, or how you ended up on this path. You haven't stopped to ask yourself what matters to you and what your own dreams are. Writing can help you uncover your dreams and bring clarity to your life goals.

Today, write about your dream life as if it's already here. Imagine that all your dreams came true, and you have achieved every goal you set for yourself. Describe what your dream life looks like. Remember that you don't have to be realistic at all. Imagine where you live, what you do, what you have, and whom you're sharing your life with. Write about what it feels like to achieve all your goals and have everything you've dreamed of. What is most important and meaningful to you now? What values do you want your life to reflect? How are you feeling? Happy? Satisfied? Disappointed? Is there anything missing? Keep reflecting for ten minutes until you find more clarity about your goals and your life's purpose.

FINDING THE GIFTS

God gave you a gift of 86,400 seconds today.
Have you used one to say, 'thank you?'

– WILLIAM ARTHUR WARD

If you are anything like me, you have probably tried asking the universe to give you something specific, thinking it will solve your problems and bring you happiness only to discover the hard way that it rarely does. It takes a wise person to realize that the meaning of gift is something other than what you want and ask for.

Life is patient enough to show you what you need to see. It doesn't give based on merit. It gives freely, like the sun that shares its warmth. That will always remain life's greatest secret. It is singing its own song and doesn't need any sheet music from you or me.

Once you've realized the narrow-mindedness and futility of asking life for specific things, you move towards appreciating what life has already given you. You slowly learn not to miss the gifts that life has deemed necessary for you, even if they don't look like gifts at first. The truth is they rarely do. They often hide under the guise of pain or misfortune, and only the wisest of us can discover the gifts of new strength they bring. If you can truly feel the beauty of this perspective, you will discover that life never stops giving, and that regardless of where you are in life right now, everything is here for you, and it has always been this way.

Today, take time to reflect on a life event that you first considered a disaster but can now see as a great gift. Reflect on the lessons you have learned from it and write about the deeper understanding or a new strength you got as a result of going through this challenge. What was the blessing in disguise? You can start with, "I never thought I could see the gift in what happened ..."

SHARING THE MOST IMPORTANT QUESTION

If the only prayer you said was thank you,
that would be enough.

– MEISTER ECKHART

R esearch shows that when we are stressed or feeling down, the most important question we can ask ourselves is, "What am I grateful for?" We don't need any help noticing the things that go wrong or that disappoint our expectations, but we tend to miss or take for granted the majority of the good things in our lives. We can afford to spend half an hour complaining to a friend, but can we afford the luxury of taking just fifteen minutes to notice and appreciate what we have, and to feel into all the things, people, experiences, and circumstances that we are grateful for?

Start small and write down three things that you feel grateful for right now. This can be something that happened today, like getting a seat on the subway or getting an excellent cup of coffee from a place you've just discovered. It can also be something that you have had in your life for years, like the support of someone close to you who cheered you on through your darkest moments. It can be something small or something big. Take a deep breath and focus on the three things that you feel grateful for right now. You can start with, "Today I am grateful for …" and freewrite for seven minutes.

If you liked writing about the things you are grateful for and are ready to reach a new level of wisdom, you could continue expanding the list to include one hundred things you are grateful for. If you can't find a hundred, write down fifty. If fifty is hard, start with twenty. If you can't find twenty, write down however many you can find right now and keep adding to your list every day, so you can get into the habit of searching your mind and heart every morning or every night for all the little things to be grateful for. You would be wise to make it a daily habit because the feelings of gratitude and appreciation will enlighten you to all the gifts you have already been given.

COLLECTING PEBBLES

Knowing yourself is the beginning
of all wisdom.

– ARISTOTLE

If we look back at our life carefully, we'll notice that we tend to collect certain kinds of experiences that are unique to each one of us. For example, some of us keep stumbling upon people who are unavailable, while others seem to be forever solving other people's problems and ignoring their own. Noticing these themes can be a challenging task. Usually, when we start feeling uncomfortable, it seems easier to avoid the situation than to face it. We think if we just stay away from this arrogant person, we won't have to find a way to deal with their arrogance. So we leave our lovers, abandon friendships, move away from a stranger on the bus, and lo and behold—there's another arrogant person waiting for us on the next bus, in the next friendship, and in the next relationship.

There's really no such thing as turning away from the messages your soul is trying to send you. The secret is to meet them fully without knowing how. The sooner you listen, the sooner you hear. The truth is life is not stacking the cards against you—it only wants to give you a message that will help you grow. It's a message from your soul. Life has no problem repeating a message or a question that you need to hear at any point in your life, and if you do your part right now, you won't have to repeat the lesson over and over.

Today, start picking up the themes, patterns, and threads in your life like you would pebbles at the beach and examine them with care one by one. It is very important that you don't judge them as you collect them. Just relax and take a stroll alongside the shore of your life. Which pebbles or shells will you find? What will the sea choose to reveal today? Which thought patterns will you come across when walking through your life history? Write about both the positive and so-called negative ones.

If you look back at the past twelve months, do you notice any themes that keep coming up? Any patterns, any questions or conflicts that keep calling to you? They may come from billboards, books, found objects, or from conversations with strangers. They might be the themes of your recurrent dreams. Try to remember them. Call them up and ask them to reveal any messages they have for you. Freewrite about them without expecting any answers or insights. For now, just give them attention and space on the page. The rest is out of your hands. You can start with, "I seem to always ..." or "I seem to never ..."

As you're writing them down, reflect on what this is about. What is it that you can't seem to hear? Try to be honest and open with yourself and write down whatever comes to you. No one needs to see this except you. This exercise is between you and your soul, so take the time to listen and allow yourself the luxury of delving deep and staying with the exercise even if it gets difficult. Don't set the time limit for this exercise. Instead, set the intention of listening within.

WRITING TO SIMPLIFY

Simplicity is the ultimate sophistication.

– LEONARDO DA VINCI

Experience tells us that overcomplicated life rarely feels good. When we come across something true or beautiful, it usually strikes us with its simplicity. It makes us feel clear, light, and spacious. The nature of the mind is to complicate things and present us with the never-ending challenges, obstacles, and to-do lists. There's nothing wrong with having a complex and nuanced perception of things. The trouble is that overcomplicated thinking can distract us from things that are truly important to us, and we can lose sight of them without even noticing.

Take a few moments to ponder the one thing in your life that is most important to you right now. This might seem impossible to choose just one because your life is full of important things. But right now, think of just one thing that's paramount. Currently, how much space does it have in your life? Is it enough for you, or would you like to give it more space? Does it figure prominently in your daily life? If it doesn't, what does? Do you attend to it every day? Why not? Where does your time go? How could you rearrange your day to make more space for it?

To look at it from another angle, which part of your life feels cluttered and overcomplicated? Which part of your life needs more breathing room in it? Which parts are you ready to let go of, and which ones would you like to clear of debris and let sparkle more? You can start with "The most important thing in my life right now is ..." and continue for seven minutes, reflecting on any of the questions above.

WRITING INTO THE
MYSTERY OF LIFE

I do not at all understand the mystery of grace—only that it meets us where we are but does not leave us where it found us.

– ANNE LAMOTT

We tend to shy away from going directly into the mystery life presents to us every now and then. Instead, we pretend to know everything. This feels safer than being vulnerable and admitting our own helplessness. Meanwhile, mystery is at the heart of this world. Revealed at the most unexpected moment, it invokes a sense of wonder and humility before the magical orchestration of it all, from the majestic beauty of the changing seasons to the shapeshifting clouds, to the perfect harmony and synchronicity of our lives.

What if instead of trying to figure out why things happen the way they do, you admitted that life is unknowable and allowed yourself to spend some time awe-struck by life? Every moment fresh. Without an author. What if instead of making plans and trying to manipulate life, you considered the narrow path of the present moment and balanced on the razor edge between the known and the unknown?

Write about some of the most perplexing things in your life right now. You can start by writing down "The biggest mystery for me right now is ..." and don't stop until seven minutes are up. Write about all those questions that don't seem to have any answers.

CHAPTER 4

RELATIONSHIP WITH NATURE

DISCOVERING THE LANGUAGE OF NATURE

*When I admire the wonders of a sunset or the
beauty of the moon, my soul expands in the
worship of the creator.*

– MAHATMA GANDHI

The natural world is so rich. Most of us tend to take it for granted and go about our day without giving it much attention. We treat it as something that is just there, in the background. Invisible. Meaningless. Unimportant. But it can teach us so much if we pause for a moment to hear all the different languages it speaks.

Mountains, oceans, fire, the sun, clouds, rain, trees, earth, sand, the sky, the stars, the moon, the wind … Each one has its own spirit that we can sense. Each one beckons us in a different way. Each one communicates a unique message. The sky looks like freedom, the stars scream mystery, the sand spells comfort, the mountains embody eternity, etc. When we identify with one of the elements, it is as if we add a missing element to our own spirit. I naturally align with water. I love the rhythm of the waves and their dynamic yet gentle music.

What about you? What natural element do you align with? Which one of the natural elements speaks to you louder than all other elements? Write about that element that speaks to your soul in this moment. What does it symbolize? What quality of nature beckons you today and gives you energy and inspiration? What about it soothes you and gives you comfort? What element does your soul need today? You can start with, "Right now my spirit needs ..." and continue for seven minutes.

LEARNING TO WRITE
FROM WATER

To have faith is to trust yourself to the water.
When you swim you don't grab hold of the
water, because if you do you will sink and
drown. Instead you relax, and float.

– ALAN WATTS

Writing has always reminded me of a running stream because of the way it flows from one thought to another. Often, we become unaware of this natural flow because we are too busy controlling it. We plan where the water should drift, outline what we are trying to say, and try to correct the current as we go. We try to arrest the flow, but we don't realize how much we stand to lose from suffocating our writing in this way.

If as an experiment we let go of the reigns and let our writing flow without judging it, we can hear our thoughts run like a stream of consciousness, watch them shapeshift like clouds and merge with one another in a seamless fashion. We might even accidentally discover some of the secrets we have kept from ourselves.

Today, allow the stream to take its course. Give it space, watch it express anything freely and fully until it runs its course and comes to a still point. Write down everything you hear running through your head right now and simply give it space on the page without judging it. Watch your mind ripple in the form of thoughts and feelings until it calms down naturally. Take as long as you need to notice the natural ebb and flow of the mind expressing itself through writing into a new stillness.

GIVING YOUR TROUBLES
TO THE RIVER

*The spirit of the universe dances to its own
tune. It connects everything—dust, rocks,
plants, animals, men, stars and galaxies—by
this mysterious rhythm. The greatest of peace
comes from surrendering to its will.*

– SRINI CHANDRA

Writing is like walking by the river. As you walk, the soothing rhythm of the stream inevitably calms you down. Your pace becomes slower, allowing you to notice the silence and the rhythm of your steps and heartbeat. Maybe the hypnotic power of the river spirit will pull you gently to sit down for a moment, slow down, put all your troubles away for a while, or better yet, give them to the water. The river knows how to set them free.

Right now, take a moment and give all your troubles to the stream of writing. Like a river, your writing can accept the gifts of worry and fear. It knows what to do with them. Give them away right now so you can be free. Soon, the stream will take them all and make them disappear beneath its dark surface. Soon, the stream will sparkle and reflect nothing but the infinite sky, sunlight and freedom, so that you can continue your walk unburdened. Take a moment to write down anything that's on your mind right now. Anything that troubles you—all of your big and little worries. You can use any of the following phrases to start with and continue for at least seven minutes:

I'm worried that …

I wonder if …

I'm concerned that …

I'm afraid that …

I fear that …

CLIMBING YOUR SECRET MOUNTAIN

It is not the mountain we conquer but
ourselves.

– EDMUND HILLARY

Mountains have traditionally been powerful symbols of spirituality and have been revered as sacred. A mountain may symbolize something different to you, but to me it means something insurmountable, unreachable, or at least, difficult to conquer. It stands for something that commands respect and requires patience, perseverance, and courage.

Facing life's challenges head on is a mountain not many of us are prepared to face. Writing about them is like climbing a mountain. It's hard to start, and even harder to stay with. The longer we climb, the harder it gets. At some point, we might feel that if we don't turn around and head back to the base camp, we will die. Given the chance, most of us would head back to safety when we are this close to the top. We might want so much to avoid facing our biggest challenges that we will choose to never even start the climb and stay safe at the base camp, pretending the mountain is not there at all. But we know our own secret mountain, and there's no running away from it or going around it.

The longer we climb, the more territory we conquer. The higher we are, the more we can feel how close we are to the top. That feeling makes us push onwards so that we can discover a new perspective that opens up only once we've reached the very top at the very end of a long journey.

And even though the road ahead is not easy and it takes courage to even acknowledge our secret mountain, most of us would still love to reach the peak where we may discover a newfound insight and wisdom.

Take a moment to explore the symbol of a mountain and imbue it with your own personal meaning. You can dive into freewriting right away or start by reflecting on any or all of the following questions, and then continue by freewriting for at least seven minutes:

Even though I am not ready now, what mountain in my life will I eventually have to climb?

What is my highest mountain made of?

What is my secret mountain that I don't share with anyone?

What do I hope to see at the top?

Which mountain remains unconquered?

WRITING TO FIND A PATH

*No one saves us but ourselves. No one can
and no one may. We ourselves must walk the
path.*

– BUDDHA

Writing is like walking alone in the forest. You find a path and follow it wherever it leads. Or you make your own path and walk into the unknown, one step at a time. Sometimes it's uphill, sometimes it's even ground, and sometimes you can barely catch your breath running down the hill. Sometimes, the path is well lit, and sometimes you have to make your way in the dark, moving only by the inner light of your faith and hope.

We so rarely pause to take a good look at our path and where it is leading us because we are either too busy walking or too busy being stuck. Today, take a closer look at the path you are on right now and give yourself a chance to discover something new.

Close your eyes for just a few moments. Imagine that you are alone in the forest. In your mind's eye, look around, take in your surroundings, and walk in any direction that draws you. Try to notice everything around you. Take in every detail and notice the sensations in your body. Now open your eyes and, while holding onto the image and feeling of the path in your mind and body, write about the unfolding path as you are walking on it in your imagination. Write for seven minutes without stopping, following the path in your imagination.

Write down everything you notice, especially if anything happens to you on the path, say, if you meet someone on the way, or if the landscape suddenly changes. If you spot a structure, like a cabin or a hut, go inside and describe everything you see. Maybe you'll observe something meaningful or symbolic, something that holds a very personal meaning to you. Keep it a secret and entrust it only to the page. You can start by writing down, "When I was standing alone in the forest, I noticed a path that was calling me. It looked … I felt …" and continue for at least seven minutes.

WRITING WITH THE RAIN

A poet is someone who stands outside in the
rain hoping to be struck by lightning.
– JAMES DICKEY

Most of the time, we see rain as a nuisance. All we can think about is that it makes us wet and cold, and so we rush inside to find shelter. Other times, however, we can see its power and its poetry. There are those rare moments when we can recognize rain as a miracle that gently brings together the sky and the earth. In this magical union, the secrets of the universe are revealed.

You don't need to be a poet to connect with ancient metaphors, imagining the skies crying or envisioning Zeus throwing lightning bolts in anger. Do we have enough perception and wisdom to recognize the mystery of the rain and listen to what it is saying? The rain is tapping each of us on the shoulder. Who will listen? And more importantly, who will hear what it's saying?

Remember the rain. Close your eyes and imagine yourself caught in the rain in some beautiful place.

Listen to the rain in your imagination. Pretend the rain is speaking to you, and to you alone. What is it trying to say to you? Why is it vying for your attention? Where in your life have you not been paying attention? What is the rain whispering to you? Can you hear the words in each drop? What do you hear? What message from life have you been refusing to hear that the rain reminds you of?

WALKING IN A SECRET GARDEN

Give me odorous at sunrise a garden
of beautiful flowers where I can walk
undisturbed.

– WALT WHITMAN

Gardens are good for the soul. They are rare spaces where time slows down and plants and trees can germinate, sprout, grow, and bear fruit in their own time. In contrast, most of us spend our days rushing and racing. Meanwhile, the beauty and the mystery of nature are there for us to observe, but we usually hurry by them so we can be more efficient and productive. I wonder if such pace is good for us.

In a garden, the city bustle is forgotten, and the daily pressure to speed up is abandoned. Gardens are spaces where we intentionally slow down and take time to admire the beauty of this world, ponder its intricate designs and the mysterious orchestration of it all. They are islands of peace and stillness, harmony and rest amidst a busy city life filled with noise and worry. Gardens are terribly important for our souls, which are constantly in search of refuge, solace, and answers.

Imagine that you are taking a stroll in a place you've never been before and stumble upon a barely visible, ancient overgrown gate, as if from a fairy tale. You open the gate and find yourself in a secret garden that looks as though it has been waiting just for you. No one else seems to notice the gate except you. Push the gate open and step inside. Try to take in everything around you as you journey through the garden. The questions below are only meant to ignite your imagination, so read through them, and once you start writing, don't try to follow or remember them. Write about any imagery they prompt so that your writing remains spontaneous and unpredictable.

Right now, focus on what you feel, see, and hear as you enter the gate. What is the feeling you get when you enter? What sounds do you hear? Are there birds? Music? The sound of wind? What is the path like? Which part of the day is it, and which season? As you stroll along the path, what thoughts are running through your head? As you wander, do you meet any strange people or creatures there? What do they look, sound, feel, and smell like? Do they communicate with you? What do they say, and what language do they speak? How do you know what they are saying?

Imagine that as the path curves around, you stumble upon something unexpected. What is it? Is there anything that looks out of place, perhaps should be removed? Is there anything that is missing? What would you change in this garden? What feeling would it give you? If you could bring someone to this secret garden of yours, whom would you bring and why? Would you walk through this secret garden once and leave or linger? For how long? Would you leave when it gets dark or stay overnight? What would make you leave? Freewrite for seven minutes.

CHAPTER 5

RELATIONSHIP
WITH YOUR WORLD

EXPLORING SUCCESS

Success is not the key to happiness. Happiness
is the key to success. If you love what you are
doing, you will be successful.

– ALBERT SCHWEITZER

All of us want to be successful. And each of us defines success in our own way. For some, success is achieving great things and leaving a legacy. Fulfilling their soul's purpose. Expressing their own creative vision with great passion and focus. For others, success is helping someone else be successful.

Explore your own vision of success before you accidentally adopt someone else's vision or succumb to the widely adopted cultural definitions of success. You want to choose your own definitions, values, and priorities so that you don't become a victim of aggressive advertisement, which imposes very certain and very suspicious visions of success. If you look inside your own heart for wisdom, you are protected from any influence, however powerful it might be.

I feel successful when I love. When I stay open and am able to give space to what is and not need to be in control. I feel successful when I'm at peace and can remain kind and tender. I used to think achieving goals and taking actions could bring me joy and freedom, but they never did. No achievements brought me any lasting sense of success or satisfaction. In fact, they were often followed by a marked frustration. These days, success means peace, love, clarity, and presence.

Think about a moment in your life when you felt successful. Is it different from what it means to be successful for you at this stage of your life? When do you feel successful these days? You can even play with developing a simple formula for success. For example: Success = courage + kindness + influence − hurting others.

You can start with, "I feel successful when …" and freewrite for seven minutes.

LEARNING FROM THE STREETS

*I'm greedy about cities—I like to form my
impressions of them on my own, and on
foot as far as possible, looking and listening,
having conversations with bridges and streets
and riverbanks, conversations I tend not to
be aware of until a little later, when I find
myself returning to those places to say hello
again, even if only in memory.*

– HELEN OYEYEMI

S treets are like people. They have different personalities and
evoke different moods. Some of them are inviting, and
some push you away the moment you set foot on them. Some
you are attracted to instantly, and others you are afraid to turn
on. Streets have plenty of secrets to share with us if we pay
attention. They can teach us a lot about ourselves as well. We
align with certain elements of theirs, like light, space, safety,
beauty, etc. They offer their space to our souls so that we can

recognize what we feel and need in this moment. So that we can choose our next step and our direction.

Try to remember some of the more memorable streets you've walked recently or when you were a child. List five to start with. What do you notice about the five streets you've listed? What do they have in common? Is there a common theme? Now, pick the most meaningful one and describe the way it looked, sounded, felt, and smelled. What were you doing? Where were you going? Did you walk down that street, sit on a bench and watch people go by, or did you lie down under a tree and look at the sky? What were you thinking and feeling? Describe that moment in your life.

WRITING TO SHED THE MASKS

The most important kind of freedom is to be
what you really are. You trade in your reality
for a role. You give up your ability to feel,
and in exchange, put on a mask.

– JIM MORRISON

asks are fake. It takes a lot of energy to maintain them, and we know it. Then why do we wear them? They must be giving us something. Otherwise, we wouldn't choose to wear them. We slip into them without noticing, and before we know it, we are already playing a role. Why do we put so much effort into constructing a specific image we want to present to the world in place of our true self? Depending on the situation, masks can make us feel useful and important. They can make us feel powerful and protected. In control. They are images we have selected to present to the world instead of our own Self and our truth.

What would happen if we showed the world who we truly are? What would be so scary about relaxing into our authentic self and not worrying about how the world sees us? We might get rejected. This fear keeps us from expressing our own true self for years, or even decades.

Take a moment to become familiar with your masks. Start by making a list of five or ten masks you wear on a regular basis. For example, here are some of mine:

Mediator

Meditator

Helper

Saviour

Hero

Martyr

Champion

Firefighter ...

Write about what each mask helps you feel. What's the worst that can happen if you put that particular mask down? Write about that too. Go through your list and reflect for seven minutes.

WRITING TO CONNECT TO YOUR WORLD

*But I'll tell you what hermits realize. If you
go off into a far, far forest and get very
quiet, you'll come to understand that you're
connected with everything.*

– ALAN WATTS

The nature of life is interconnectedness. There's nothing that exists separately from the rest of life. Including ourselves. Sometimes we lose sight of this simple truth. Instead we imagine that we are a small person, separate from everything and everyone, who, therefore, needs to constantly defend themselves against the world. This separation is a powerful illusion that can affect our beliefs, attitudes, words, and actions. It's fairly easy to slip into this illusion because we rarely, if ever, take the time to feel all the connections we enjoy in our lives.

Through writing, we can discover and appreciate all the ways we connect to the world.

Start by drawing a figure of yourself in the middle of a blank page. It can be a stick figure, a smiley face, a heart, or the letter "I". It's only for your eyes. No one else needs to see it. Now, draw ten lines radiating from the centre, each representing one important connection in your life. At the end of the line, write down what it represents. For example, each line might represent your connection with your family, friends, pet, health, spirituality, community, country, career, passion, etc. Write down what's important to you alone.

Take another piece of paper and, again, draw yourself in the middle of the page. Around your figure, write down all the things, people, places, qualities, feelings that you'd like to be connected to but are currently not. It might be a lost childhood friend, an abandoned hobby, your spirit, a new path in life, self-compassion, etc. Try to be specific and explore the things and people you'd like to be (re) connected with. Now, slowly and deliberately draw thick lines connecting the figure of yourself in the middle of the page to each and every one of these new things and people you have placed on the page around you. You might choose different colours and line designs that symbolize how you feel about these new connections. After you're done, freewrite about anything you noticed during the process. What thoughts went through your mind? What feelings and emotions? Don't think ahead—surprise yourself by what you discover.

EXPLORING OWNERSHIP

Happiness resides not in possessions, and not in gold, happiness dwells in the soul.

– DEMOCRITUS

A sense of ownership is such a strange thing. We are convinced we can own something. We are driven to acquire and collect things, but can we really own them? Ownership is most commonly expressed by the verb "to have", and our daily use of this word is even more peculiar. The expression "I have" implies a simplified model of relationship and does not reflect the complexity of the actual dynamic. We are used to saying, "I have a friend" or "I have a family", but do we really have a friend? What does it mean to own or to have something or someone?

While we may think we own something, some things start owning us before we even realize it. Our sense of ownership is worth investigating. We might find a broader perspective and recognize some patterns and threads that we seem to gravitate towards.

Think of three possessions that you cherish and feel you wouldn't be able to part with. What do they mean to you? What do they symbolize? Freewrite about the special meaning each one has in your heart. What do they make you feel, and which need of yours do they fulfill? Write for at least seven minutes before you move on to the next exercise.

Explore three of your own qualities that you cherish and wouldn't want to change. How did they become yours? How did you come to possess them? Who gave them to you? Did you notice them in others before they became yours? Whom did you admire for having these qualities? Write for seven minutes.

Write about three intangible things you enjoy but can't own. For example, friends. You can't really own them, but you can still enjoy, cherish, and appreciate them fully. Think of other things you truly enjoy without owning, and freewrite for seven minutes.

QUESTIONING A SENSE OF LACK

> *Wealth consists not in having great possessions, but in having few wants.*
>
> – EPICTETUS

I f our sense of ownership is a strange thing, our sense of lack is even more suspicious. It often manifests as a habit of shopping for perfection. Somehow, probably unconsciously, we must believe that getting the right thing will help us fill an imaginary hole and make us happy. It's quite funny if you stop to think about it. Rationally, we know that nothing we acquire can change the way we feel. But in our daily life, we often act to the contrary. We delude ourselves into believing that in order to feel whole and complete, we need to get that thing that will magically make us feel complete. This false yet pervasive sense of lack is worth investigating.

What are you lacking that you are constantly shopping for? What do you feel is missing in your life right now? Is it a perfect husband, a perfect vacation, or a perfect outfit? A perfect gift, a perfect pet, a perfect job? Maybe a perfect path in life? Write about the perfect thing(s) you feel you "need" in order to be happy at this stage of your life. What do those perfect things you "need" symbolize to you? Safety? Success? Achievement? What can they tell you about yourself? How are they promising to make you happy, whole, and complete? Write for at least seven minutes.

CLAIMING YOUR TREASURES

Ordinary riches can be stolen; real riches cannot. In your soul are infinitely precious things that cannot be taken from you.

– OSCAR WILDE

We are all rich beyond measure. If you are reading this, then you have been given a life. We have the capacity to love and to forgive, to be kind and true. But we so rarely stop to acknowledge things that we have. It's like using a treasure chest as a stool to sit on and never opening it to notice the treasure. It's both funny and a little sad. Today is the day we take a moment to notice our riches and open the chest we've been sitting on and claim our fortune.

What are your riches right now? Reflect on what you treasure most in your life. What treasures have you already collected in your heart? Make a list. What do you cherish the most? These can be experiences, strengths, abilities, people, character traits, etc. Pick one and freewrite about it for seven minutes before you move on to the next part of writing.

Now that you have claimed your fortune, you can enjoy building your very own and very special treasure chest to keep all your treasures safe. What does it look like? What shape does it have? What colour? What is it made of? Cotton candy? Pure crystal? Gold? How would you keep it away from anyone's eyes? Would you hide it in the clouds? Is it levitating under the ceiling in your bedroom and becomes invisible once anyone opens the door? Is it sitting up in your favourite treetop? Buried at the bottom of the sea? Let your imagination go and honour your treasures by giving them an appropriate place to live. Write for seven minutes.

Now that you have built your special treasure chest and filled it with the treasures that you've collected up to now, reflect on what other five treasures you would love to add to it in the near future. Write for seven minutes.

CHAPTER 6

RELATIONSHIP
WITH PAIN

WRITING TO VENT

*Whatever sorrow shakes from your heart, far
better things will take their place.*

– RUMI

At times, all of us could use a good venting session. It feels good to get it all out of our system, to unload, to air all our complaints about the world and other people. Nothing is wrong with that, as long as we don't overload our friends or family with our venting. And as long as we don't take our grievances too seriously or get stuck in them.

Often, our venting has a destructive element to it, so when we vent to others, even if they love and care for us, their patience might eventually run out. It can also be emotionally taxing for them. In this way, writing is a perfect medium for venting because it allows you to avoid these negative circumstances, collect your thoughts about the situations that you perceive as negative, and reflect on them once they are captured on paper. You don't have to filter what you are saying, so you can be completely honest because you are not going to hurt anyone's feelings. And you can still experience the therapeutic value of expressing yourself without compromising your relationships with your loved ones.

Make a list of all the things that are causing you to suffer right now. They can be petty and ridiculous, selfish and unfair. In fact, it's great if they are. It means that you are being honest with yourself. If you are already thinking and feeling them, you might as well take a look at what's going on inside. Do your best to not judge them as you write them down. Allow yourself to be childish, whiny, unfair, and make these grievances as subjective and unreasonable as possible. Do not filter. It will make the next part of this exercise more fun. But no peeking ahead until you're done with your venting.

For the second part of this exercise, write a response from your wiser and older parent self to the part of you that needed the venting. Respond with kindness and compassion. Try to find a way to accept and appreciate whatever it is that you're struggling with. Imagine that your inner child is complaining to you and speak to them with compassion and kindness. Take seven minutes to write your responses.

QUITTING THE AVOIDANCE GAME

> *Laws of silence don't work... When*
> *something is festering in your memory or*
> *your imagination, laws of silence don't work,*
> *it's just like shutting a door and locking it on*
> *a house on fire in hope of forgetting that the*
> *house is burning. But not facing a fire doesn't*
> *put it out. Silence about a thing just magnifies*
> *it. It grows and festers in silence, becomes*
> *malignant.*
>
> – TENNESSEE WILLIAMS

Each of us is afraid to face some situations or people for fear of failure, success, appearing foolish or weak. It's normal to want to avoid things we don't want to face, but the truth is that we can't avoid them forever. We all know it because we have tried to do it, but we quickly learned that the more we try, the more viciously those unwanted memories, people, and situations attack our minds. Facing what we have been avoiding requires a lot of courage. It requires paying attention to what our bodies have been trying to say to us. It also requires self-care and preparation. Luckily, writing can provide all of these elements.

Wait until you can dedicate some uninterrupted time and make your writing spot as comfortable as possible. You can light a candle, get a cup of tea, or your favourite drink, take a few deep breaths, and connect to your heart. Ask yourself what you have been avoiding, be it a person, a situation or a feeling. Maybe a memory. Invite it in and pay close attention to what comes. Write everything down. If you don't know how to start, you can write down the question itself, "What am I afraid to tackle? What am I afraid to remember, understand, or forgive?" and write for as long as you need.

WELCOMING THE MESSENGER

Grief can be the garden of compassion. If you
keep your heart open through everything, your
pain can become your greatest ally in your
life's search for love and wisdom.

– RUMI

When pain shows up, we tend to run away. We do whatever is possible to deny it and push it aside. We are scared of what it has to say and what we have to do after being confronted. We are scared to feel it and will do anything to distract ourselves.

But if you look closely, you will notice that our fear of pain is actually preventing us from experiencing the pain fully. Because we don't let it in, we never hear its message. If you drop your fear of pain, you will see that pain is not an enemy. It can become a friend and a messenger. If you tell the truth, you will have to admit that you are larger than the pain. You own the house whose door it knocks on, and you can let it onto your porch without forgetting your power. And since pain is your guest right now, you do not have to forget your hospitality. You can bow to it and show it in.

This one time, just as an experiment, do not shut the door when the pain comes. Do not run or push it away. Try greeting the pain at the door and welcoming it.

This time, feel it fully. Attend openly to what it has come to tell you and listen to what it needs from you. Give it the best seat in the house of your heart and ask it what it wants to tell you. Listen patiently. Allow yourself to go deeper. Thank life for sending this messenger to share something important with you, something life needs you to hear. Life must have trust that this time, you can hear the pain and not push it away.

Start by taking a deep breath and ask the pain, "What message do you bring me today? What do you need me to hear?" and for seven minutes, write down whatever comes to mind.

WRITING TO LICK
THE WOUNDS

*Our sorrows and wounds are healed only
when we touch them with compassion.*

– BUDDHA

When animals are wounded, they don't pretend they're not. They don't rush to get up and run again. They stay with the pain. They take the time and space they need to heal. They don't ignore their wound but give it their full attention. They can lick it for hours at a time, with love and care. We can learn from animals. Pretending to be okay never helped anyone. It is okay to feel our wounds and "lick" them gently until they heal. And there is no better way to heal our wounds than through writing.

Divide the page into two columns and make two lists. In the first one, list all the wounds that you feel ready to heal. In the other column, list all the wounds that are still infected and are too painful to touch at this time. Leave them for now and start with the wounds that are easier to work through. Pick one wound you would like to heal and answer any of the following questions. Where in your body do you feel the wound? Don't think about it and focus on sensations only. Is it in your back, your neck, or your jaw? Do you feel tightness in your chest or heaviness in your head? Is your chest pumping, or your heart throbbing? Is the whole body feeling heavier? Write for five minutes before you move onto the next part of writing.

Staying with the same wound, remember the exact moment when you got hurt. How did your body feel the moment you were wounded? Did you feel like you got punched in the stomach, or your knees gave way, or your spine snapped in two? Could you taste tears in your throat? Write what you remember even if you don't remember all the details.

What did you want to do physically the moment you got wounded? Did you want to cry, scream, punch a wall, or punch the person who hurt you? Did you want to break something? Throw something across the room? Slap the person across the face? Shut the door in their face? Don't be afraid of the violent images. Write it all out of your system. What do you wish you had said to the person who broke your heart, caused you harm, or hurt someone you love? If there was no person involved, talk to life, God, or the universe about your feelings. Write a letter to the person, God, or universe articulating your feelings about what happened, and read it out loud. Be sure to express yourself honestly and completely and hear yourself out with love and compassion. If you feel uncomfortable keeping what you wrote, you can always delete or burn it afterwards.

DEALING WITH
A GHOSTLY VISIT

*Sorrow prepares you for joy. It violently
sweeps everything out of your house, so that
new joy can find space to enter. It shakes the
yellow leaves from the bough of your heart,
so that fresh, green leaves can grow in their
place. It pulls up the rotten roots, so that new
roots hidden beneath have room to grow.*

– RUMI

Not all wounds are ready to be healed. We all have memories we are afraid to revisit. They are just too painful. We feel that if we touch them, we might explode and die. But I promise that won't be the case. It's just our ego that feels threatened. Why are we so afraid to recall a specific memory? We're afraid to open a Pandora's box that we will be unable to close. We are afraid of becoming overwhelmed by feelings of sadness, regret, confusion, uncertainty, and grief. So we erroneously believe that the best solution is to deny our feelings.

What are some things from the past that you are not yet ready to revisit? What if these old ghosts came knocking without asking whether you're ready or not? Could you let them in without panicking or freaking out? Are you able to allow them a place in your life? Freewrite about why it's better to keep them out of your life for now. Write about what you are afraid might happen if you opened the door to those memories and let them into your life. You can start with, "I am afraid to remember or think about the time when … because …" and continue for seven minutes.

WRITING TO LET GO

Some of us think holding on makes us strong;
but sometimes it is letting go.

– HERMANN HESSE

Some things we hold on to are not good for us, and we can feel it. Yet we still hold on to them. Why on earth, you ask? No clue, except that it's a very human thing to do. We are clear that we don't want to behave, think, or feel in certain ways, but we find ourselves doing it on autopilot. We don't know what to do, so the best solution we've come up with is to keep the same habits. Writing is our chance to dance with these precious tokens of the past one last time, hold them in our arms, thank them one by one, give each one of them one last kiss, and let them go.

Today, try something before you start writing. For just one moment, close your eyes and completely relax the muscles of your face, scalp, eyes, jaw, neck, shoulders, chest, back, abdomen, arms, hands, legs, feet. For ten seconds, notice what it feels like to release all tension from your body and to relax fully.

What other tensions are you willing to let go of? What habits of the mind or the body no longer serve you and need to be released? Are there any unhelpful or toxic things that you are ready to let go of? Are there people, places, circumstances that no longer serve your life and need to go?

You can start with, "I am ready to let go of ..." and write non-stop for at least seven minutes, or longer if you wish. You don't have to rush this. Spend as much time as you need with the things you're letting go of. Thank each one of them for coming into your life as a friend to help you find a certain kind of strength, learn a new lesson, or uncover a new freedom. Reflect and write about these strengths, lessons, and freedom they have given you.

Now that you worked hard on letting go of the things, habits, and people that no longer serve you, as a reward, you get to write about what you would like to welcome into your life instead. Make a fresh start, open a symbolic door, lay out a welcome mat, and start inviting any guests you want. You can begin with, "I am ready to welcome ..." and continue for seven minutes.

WRITING TO HEAL

The wound is the place where the Light

enters you.

– RUMI

Sometimes, writing about our memories can feel like touching old wounds. Some of them have healed completely so we can write about them peacefully, without hurting. Some wounds are still healing, and writing about them feels soothing because we give them our undivided loving attention and care.

Understandably, our instinct is to write around the pain. To write about the ways to heal, to forgive and forget. But what would happen if we wrote about the pain directly by describing all its facets? In my experience, the pain intensifies for a little bit, and you can feel the fire growing, but soon the pain begins to fade. And, often, it disappears completely. Could you find the courage it takes to walk right through the fire of pain? Not around it. Without wishing it away. What if you went into the unknown and accepted the benevolence of the fire?

Is it possible for you to find a way to trust that the fire is not here to burn you but only to burn off the excess that is untrue? Can you trust that it is here to show you your distorted perception of the situation and your unhelpful beliefs? The moment you can accept and honour the graceful fire of pain, you have prepared the ground for the miracle of healing to happen.

Right now, do not analyze your pain. Do not question or judge it. Your only task for now is to express your pain to yourself. Just that. Without asking why or trying to understand it, put down on paper every little hurt you feel right now. You can start by writing, "Today I'm hurting because …" and write it all out for at least seven minutes. You might want to do something soothing after you finish writing, like taking a walk or a bath.

WRITING TO FIND REST

*Most of the things we need to be most fully
alive never come in busyness.
They grow in rest.*

– MARK BUCHANAN

We all need rest from pain. Every now and then, we need to be able to leave all burdens, goals, and agendas behind and simply rest in the present moment. Writing is a permanent invitation to be right here right now and to rest in your being. Not reaching into the past or the future. Staying with what is here in front of you. Face to face. Choosing to act or not to—whichever is truer in the moment.

Writing helps you meet yourself where you are. It invites you to return to yourself and not leave yourself for anyone or anything. Standing in the centre of this moment and resting … just like this … exactly as you are right now. Not interpreting this moment but meeting it in your fullness. How many goals do you need to accomplish to be more of yourself? How many tasks do you need to finish to feel complete? How many more moments to become yourself? And where do you need to go in order to feel that you have arrived? Where is the stopping point? Is there ever a stopping point?

Take a moment to find out what your relationship with rest is. You can begin by replying to the following questions without much preparation. Just follow your mind and don't stop to reread or rethink what you've written. For now, just collect your thoughts like precious jewels.

When was the last time I felt fully rested?

Why haven't I let myself rest in the past week, past month, past year?

Why do I need to always go faster?

Where am I going? What reward is awaiting me "there"?

What does my heart need to be able to rest right now?

Where is the resting place for my soul in this moment?

What would it take for me to let go of everything for just one moment and rest right here?

What would happen if I let myself rest right now?

When you have finished, stop completely and rest right here. Freewrite about your relationship with rest. You can begin by saying, "When I think of rest, I feel …" and freewrite for at least seven minutes.

120

CHAPTER 7

RELATIONSHIP WITH
RHYTHMS OF LIFE

DISCOVERING THE RHYTHM OF YOUR LIFE

The butterfly counts not months but moments,

and has time enough.

– RABINDRANATH TAGORE

Each of us moves through life at our own pace. Some of us speed up through each day and manage to do a thousand things every twenty-four hours. Others take time to smell the roses and appreciate the world around them. They might sit on the beach and cloud watch for hours at a time. Every life has a unique pace and rhythm. For some people, life revolves around a daily rhythm of getting the kids ready for school and then dashing to a hundred after-school activities. Some people move from one book to another. Others measure their life in stages, such as the places they lived. For example, twenty years in their parents' home and then four years in college, or two years abroad.

The rhythms of our lives change all the time. Right now, our life can feel slower than five years ago, or it can feel as though it's speeding up as we anticipate an upcoming wedding or a big birthday celebration. We are not always attuned to the rhythm of our life, but we could be more understanding and compassionate if we discovered our own rhythm and honoured it.

Take a snapshot of your life right now. At this moment, what is the typical rhythm of your day, your week, and your year? What seems to be the rhythm of your life? Do you measure your life in days, annual visits home, birthdays, weekends, books, seasons? How do you usually mark the passage of time? You can start with, "Lately, the rhythm of my life has been …" and write for seven minutes.

DESIGNING A MORNING RITUAL

When you arise in the morning, think of what
a precious privilege it is to be alive—to breathe,
to think, to enjoy, to love.

– MARCUS AURELIUS

Many people say that the first two hours of the day have the power to change our lives. They swear that the focus and productivity you can achieve in the early morning hours are unparalleled. But who has time in the morning, right? Many of us get up, sleepwalk through our morning chores, and rush out the door with coffee in hand before we are fully awake. We find it challenging to spend any time in the morning tending to anything that is truly important to us.

What if by magic, you got two extra hours added to your morning? What would you do with that time? What ritual could you invent to help you enjoy each day more fully and propel your life in the direction you want? You can start with, "If I had two extra hours every morning, the first thing I'd do is ..." and write for seven minutes.

SPRING CLEANING

All the art of living lies in a fine mingling of
letting go and holding on.

– HAVELOCK ELLIS

O ur contemporary culture puts a special focus on getting something from life. "What's in it for me?" is a popular question driving many decisions and actions. We are conditioned to acquire. As a result, hoarding and obesity have become symptoms of our times. We have been convinced that more is better.

At the same time, if you are lucky, you have experienced that giving and letting go can bring as much happiness as getting. Discovering the space of your emptiness rather than the space you can fill with possessions and food might reveal more about who you are. After all, how many possessions can you stuff into your space, and how much food will you put into your body before you discover how empty those possessions and food really feel? Emptiness and mystery are most filling and taste like dessert. In many cultures, people perform rituals that involve giving and letting go. People burn things, send them floating down the river, offer them to the universe, etc.

Today use writing to discover what you can live without. What can you let go of daily? What about each season? Physically, emotionally, mentally, and spiritually. Take seven minutes and design a daily letting go ritual. How could you let go of each day and its trials, its multiple lists and emotional upheavals? It could involve burning a candle, an incense, sage, or writing down on a piece of paper all the unhelpful things and beliefs you wish to let go of and burning it. What could a weekly, a monthly or an annual clearing look like? You can find the rhythm that works best for your life. Start exploring your letting go ritual by saying, "For my daily clearing ritual, I could … Every week, I could … Every month, I could … Every season, I could … Every year, I would love to …" and continue for seven minutes.

WRITING TO START FRESH

Each night, when I go to sleep, I die. And the next morning, when I wake up, I am reborn.

– MAHATMA GANDHI

I f you are like me, at one time or another, you got stuck in a rut. You found yourself automatically doing the same thing over and over again before you realized that a new beginning was possible, and a more creative approach was overdue. The good news is that once you recognize that you're in a rut, you can break free from the routine that got you into that rut in the first place. You can take a step back and reevaluate your goals, find new meaning, and reimagine your direction. Today you could start all over again and do everything differently.

Right now, look back at this day and imagine redoing it from scratch. Imagine that you just woke up and opened your eyes.

What time is it? What do you want to do first? What do you wish you had done differently this morning? What do you wish you had not done today at all? Spend seven minutes writing before engaging with the next part of the exercise.

Now, imagine that New Year's Eve has arrived, and you're at a party. In the midst of all the chatter and music, you excuse yourself, taking your glass with you, and sneak into a dark, empty room for some quiet. You sit on a large windowsill and peer out at the busy street outside. Take a moment to dream about the coming year and what you hope will come out of it. Imagine both the things that you would like to do by yourself and the gifts you would like to receive from the universe. Make your wishes, write down your hopes and intentions for this year. If it is mid-year already, think about events that transpired that you would like to have handled differently if you had a second chance. Now is your chance to write out a different scenario and reflect on it. What feeling would it give you, and what would it mean to you if things had unfolded the way you imagined them just now? Freewrite for seven minutes before moving to the next prompt.

And now, imagine it is the first day of your life. You don't even know yourself or the world yet. Imagine yourself as a soul that just turned up in this tiny helpless body. Make a wish for this little person. What are your hopes and intentions for this being? Write down your hopes and dreams, wishes and intentions for yourself as a little baby, starting this life fresh. Write a letter to this beautiful creature you see, and share anything you want them to know about starting this life anew.

MAKING TIME FOR RENEWAL

To be worn out is to be renewed.

– LAO TZU

Each of us has a lot to give. All day long, we share ourselves with others and give away what we have inside—love, energy, empathy, etc. But the amount of energy we have to give is finite, and inevitably, there comes a time when the well is empty, the battery is dead, and we need to recharge and get our well re-filled. If you are anything like me, you often miss that moment in time and might find yourself feeling irritated, empty, tired, and depleted without knowing why.

What if you didn't have to miss the moment when it's time to recharge? What if you could become more attuned to that moment approaching? Writing can allow you to cultivate your attention and find a better balance between expending your energy and accepting the gifts of vitality from life, your loved ones, and special places that replenish your energy.

Right now, take a moment to reflect on what you need in order to replenish your energy. Ask yourself what you need in order to feel renewed. Whether it's listening to the waves, meditating, or taking an afternoon nap that allows you to recharge completely, write about what renews your energy and makes you feel brand new. You can write about people, pets, places, or activities that give you energy. And you can start by saying, "When I am feeling exhausted, what I need is ..." and continue for seven minutes.

MOVING WITH THE RHYTHM
OF THE WEEK

*Figure out the rhythm of life and live in
harmony with it.*

– LAO TZU

Each week is different and unpredictable. Each week has its own rhythm. It speeds up and slows down. It's alive and has its own logic. Most of us have something that we love doing weekly. It's the part of the week that we look forward to the most. We like the familiarity, the comfort, and the certainty of this time that we've learned to savour every week.

You might like to run ten miles on the weekend, or volunteer at a local humane society one night a week. You might love going for a long walk on the waterfront on Sunday morning, or curling up on the couch with a book or to watch a movie on a Saturday night.

What is your favourite part of the week? What do you look forward to the most every week? You can start by saying, "My favourite part of the week is when ..." and freewrite for seven minutes.

RIDING A TRAIN

Be happy for this moment. This moment is
your life.

– OMAR KHAYYAM

There's something soothing about things that have rhythm—music, poetry, trains, waves, dancing. Writing is like riding a train. We use our pen to move with the rhythm of our thoughts and feelings. We slowly get entrained by the rhythm of the moving pen. As we write, we notice what appears before the windows of our eyes in the present moment. We become aware of what each moment consists of emotionally, spiritually, mentally, and psychologically. We get attuned to ourselves.

Life is speeding by, and each view only appears for one brief moment and disappears without a trace. The scenes are replacing one another and pretending to be important. They ask for our attention as they are passing us by. Life is here, right here, in each window, in each moment.

Imagine that you are riding a train. Describe its movement. Is it smooth and peaceful or rough and rocky? Look through the window. What do you see passing by? What kind of landscape? What kind of weather? What kind of trees? Do you spot people or animals, buildings, mountains, or an ocean? What do they look like? What are they saying to you about your life? What is the feeling of this moment? Take a snapshot of each moment and write it down as precisely as possible. You can start with, "Right now, I see ..." and continue for seven minutes.

CHAPTER 8

RELATIONSHIP
WITH TIME

TIME TRAVELLING

Let your life lightly dance on the edges of
Time like dew on the tip of a leaf.
– RABINDRANATH TAGORE

T ime travel is an attractive concept to most of us. Sometimes we dream about going back in time to get a second chance at something important that we didn't get right the first time— wishing we could take back our careless words, stand up for ourselves, hug someone we love a little longer, etc. Other times, we wish we could see into the future—wondering if it's worth going down that path, investing in this relationship, accepting that job.

I'm not a science buff and don't know how likely time travel is, but I know that writing is a perfectly suitable time machine. It can take you anywhere in time. And if your thoughts are stuck in reliving the past, writing can also get you out of there. Today, I invite you to take three journeys through time and connect hope with wisdom, innocence with experience, and aspirations with truth.

First, write a letter to your ninety-year-old self. Express your hopes and dreams for the future and ask any questions about life your older self has lived. You can begin with, "Dear ..." and freewrite for seven minutes.

After your letter is complete, write a response from your ninety-year-old self. Find out what they want to share with you at this moment. After all, your older self has learned quite a bit and can share life's many lessons and secrets. Allow your older self to give you any advice and encouragement for this moment in your journey.

After you finish your first two letters, write a letter to your five-year-old self. Write about anything you were confused or scared by, anything you were curious or unsure about. Try to give them some love, comfort, and compassion and maybe even some answers using your experience and present understanding of things that they once couldn't comprehend. You can start in the same way by saying, "Dear ..." and continue for seven minutes.

You can continue this exercise by writing to yourself at any age, especially, if there was something that bothered or confused you at that time, something you had questions about. It might also be fun to intuit and write a reply. Enjoy your very own time travelling machine and play with it as often as you would like.

REPACKING YOUR SUITCASE

*Unnecessary possessions are unnecessary
burdens. If you have them, you have to
take care of them! There is great freedom
in simplicity of living. It is those who have
enough but not too much who are the happiest.*

– PEACE PILGRIM

We are all on a journey from the past to the future. We have been travelling for a while, and most of the time, we have been carrying the same luggage with us from place to place—out of habit, really, since it's already packed and we are used to the familiar items inside. When was the last time you emptied your suitcase and reevaluated everything? Are you carrying something that used to be useful years ago but no longer serves you? Have you been oblivious about carrying something heavy that has been dragging you down and you no longer need? Now is a good moment to repack your suitcase.

140

If you could only pack five things for the near future, whether it's for next month, next six months, or next year, whom or what would you need and why? List things, people, qualities, experiences, strengths, values, beliefs, attitudes, etc. that you would like to take with you on your journey.

After you've completed your first list, reflect on the five things you've been carrying with you but didn't find useful. What five things or people would you like to unpack right now and not carry on your back one more day? When you are done with the second list, reflect on both lists. You can start with, "What surprised me the most was …" or "What I noticed was …" and continue for seven minutes.

WRITING TO COMPLETE

Write out of love. Your piece will finish itself.

– A.D. POSEY

It's not a big deal to have unfinished projects. Each of us has a few projects in progress at any given time. But there are two kinds of unfinished projects, and they are a world apart. The first kind is very simple—you either don't have time, the right tool, or the right person to help you finish. But you are clear on what it takes to finish the project. The other kind is more complicated, and you are usually unsure as to why you can't finish it. This second kind of unfinished project is worth investigating, and writing can help you shed more light on it.

Think of something that you keep trying to complete but never seem to be able to. Write down what it is. Is it something worth completing, or something you don't have the guts to let go of? Do you really want to finish it, or can you uncover a hidden reason why you prefer not to? What scares you about completing it? Are you afraid of what's next, or that it won't be perfect? Is it in conflict with your self-image? Stay with your thoughts for a while and see if all of your fears about completing it are still valid, or if there are some fears you are ready to release?

Is there anything that still excites you about completing this project, or is it an expired dream? Remember how you felt in the beginning of the project, and how you couldn't wait to start it. Does it still feel as exciting, or are you trying to revive something that is no longer alive? How does writing about this project feel in your body? Are you excited and full of energy, or are you stuck and dragging your pen, at a loss for what to say? Observing your bodily reactions could give you a clue as to whether you still want to complete what you've started or let it go. What would it mean for you to finish it? What would it mean not to? Do you have everything you need to complete it? Who can help you get it? What are the steps you need to take to finish it? What is the first tiny step you can take right now?

MAKING TIME DISAPPEAR

When the path ignites a soul, there's no
remaining in place.
The foot touches ground, but not for long.

– HAKIM SANAI

Time is a funny thing. It can feel very different from moment to moment. Sometimes, weeks speed by, and we barely notice. Other times, hours stand still. You might be a passive observer of the moment. Or, you could be deeply engaged in dancing with life. You might be playing piano, talking on the phone with a loved one, hiking, jogging, etc. It is as if you disappear into your actions. The actions themselves become the only reality. No thoughts—just your quiet mind and the dance of the present moment. Those are rare and precious moments that teach us connection and presence.

What is it exactly that makes you forget about time? Write about the last time you were so fully engaged in doing something that you lost track of time, and even of yourself. What were you doing, and how did you feel during the activity and after you realized how much time had gone by? What was it exactly that made you forget about time? Why did that happen? Was it your passion, creativity, sense of wonder, or joy that made time disappear? You can start with, "I remember completely losing track of time when …" and continue for seven minutes.

WRITING THIS MOMENT

Do not dwell in the past, do not dream of the future, concentrate the mind on the present moment.

– BUDDHA

This moment is the only one we have, but we often miss it because our attention is somewhere else. We are revisiting things from the past or stressing about the future. But the present moment has nothing to do with either the past or future. It consists of our feelings and sensations, our emotions and our present state of mind.

Normally, we give no or very little space and attention to these subtle aspects of the present moment. We are too far removed from it, so we miss it. We miss the now of our lives. Consistently. Habitually. Unconsciously. Writing allows us to bring our full attention to the present moment and honour it.

For the next seven minutes, check in with yourself and freewrite about the way you feel right now in this moment. Explore your feelings, thoughts, physical sensations, your emotional state, and anything else that comes into your awareness. Declutter your mind and get it all out on paper. Give your full awareness to this moment as your pen is touching the page. What does it feel like to be you in this moment? You can start your response with, "Right now, I feel ..."

CALLING YOUR DARK SECRETS FROM UNDER THE BED

Shame is a soul eating emotion.

– C.G. JUNG

There are so many things we keep inside. We are ashamed of them and, therefore, unable to ask for help. So they turn into poison, eroding our soul from inside. We judge them for being unfathomable, unacceptable, and shameful. We judge ourselves for having these thoughts and feelings, thus devaluing them and denying them their right to exist. What if we welcomed them and gave them space? What if we listened? What if we simply allowed ourselves to feel what we feel and notice what is there without judging it?

Make a list of the things you are hiding from everyone because you feel ashamed of them. If you don't feel comfortable putting them on paper in plain language, feel free to use abbreviations. You can also burn the list later so that no one ever has to see it. Write for seven minutes.

Working through things is not easy. It is normal to feel tempted to run away from the issues instead of face them. Remember that the heart is powerful and can handle anything. So, allow anything to come. Just this one time, be welcoming, opening, accepting towards everything that has been in hiding, afraid to rise to the surface. Experience the sweet surrender of your self-image to the reality of life that is true and gracious. Each moment is full to the brim and brings relief. You can destroy your draft afterwards.

For the second part of this exercise, explore all your dark passions that you are afraid to feel. Sweep them out from under the bed and let them out of hiding. As an experiment, tell them it's safe to come out and show their face. What are you secretly curious about? What do you wish you didn't desire and yet secretly wish to explore? Use your own code so that you're not afraid to reveal them to the world. No one ever needs to know that you did this exercise except you. You deserve to know and to welcome all parts of yourself. Even those that scare you to death, even those you have never understood. All of them. Most of all, you deserve the freedom from shame. You can start with, "I don't understand it, but I've always been curious about …" and write for seven minutes. You can also try, "If I didn't feel so ashamed, I would …"

REWRITING THE PAST

We write to taste life twice, in the moment
and in retrospect.

– ANAÏS NIN

All of us have experienced situations we didn't like. We might have acted prematurely or in a state of shock or panic. We might not have chosen the best action or the right words in the moment, and we have been feeling guilty ever since. With the magical power of writing, we can rewrite any situation and imagine a different action and outcome. Imagining different words, different actions, and different results can award us with a new perception on the situation and change the way we have been feeling since it happened.

Think of a situation where you didn't like your words or actions and have regretted them ever since. Write about what happened and what you felt in the moment. Rewrite the situation with the wisdom and insight that you have today. You can use the following phrases if it helps you work through the situation:

When I first realized that ... I felt ...

I did what I did, but what I really wanted to do was ...

I said what I said, but I really wish I'd said ...

Write out a completely new scenario for seven minutes. After you finish, reflect on what you felt as you were rewriting. What did this new scenario allow you to feel about yourself and the others involved? What did you learn from rewriting the past?

CHAPTER 9

RELATIONSHIP
WITH CHANGE

WRITING THROUGH
A METAMORPHOSIS

The real voyage of discovery is not in seeking
new landscapes, but in having new eyes.

– MARCEL PROUST

Writing has the power to change the way you see anything by focusing your attention on it. It can transform your world. More importantly, it can transform who you are. It allows you to see through the false images of yourself and recognize your true nature.

Writing is like having wings. It lifts you up when you are at the very bottom and don't know how to get up. It can teach you how to fly if you let it, but you must learn to trust it first. You must learn to write without thinking. And without knowing how to. Is there a more powerful transformation than changing the way we see ourselves?

Today you can use writing to play the shapeshifting game. You can become anything at all without losing your true essence. The most important thing about this exercise is to write down your initial thoughts, images, and symbols without much pre-thought. This way you get to surprise yourself and make true discoveries. You are not writing to commit to a chosen image for life. You are simply checking in with yourself and choosing an image suitable for this one moment. Try to find an appropriate metaphor to symbolize how you feel right now, without judging or questioning it. The more honest you are, the more discoveries you will be able to make about who you are and who you want to be. All you have to do is finish the following sentences as quickly as you can:

If I were a season, I would be …

If I were an animal, I would be …

If I were a shape, I would be …

If I were a holiday, I would be …

If I were a building, I would be …

If I were a colour, I would be …

If I were a tree, I would be …

If I were a landscape, I would be …

If I were a piece of clothing, I would be …

If I were a piece of furniture, I would be …

If I were a drink, I would be …

If I were a fabric, I would be …

If I were a food, I would be …

If I were a movie genre, I would be …

If I were a part of the day, I would be …

Take seven minutes to reflect on the answers that surprised you the most. Now is your opportunity to go deeper and discover the reasons behind each metaphor.

EXPLORING THE CHANGING

Life is a series of natural and spontaneous changes. Don't resist them; that only creates sorrow. Let reality be reality. Let things flow naturally forward in whatever way they like.

– LAO TZU

All of us change all the time. We change our habits, preferences, attitudes, decisions, and activities. We change what we value, how we spend our time, and how we define ourselves and others. Some changes are obvious, and others might go unnoticed for quite some time. Writing can allow us to become aware of these invisible changes so that we can consciously decide whether we like them or would like to change back to the way things were.

Reflect on the changes in your life by finishing the sentences below. Write about what you used to do, feel, think, say to notice how you have changed. Finish the following sentences as many times as you'd like. After you are finished, freewrite about one or two of the changes that you feel need more reflection.

I used to … but now …

I used to be … but now …

I used to feel … but now …

I used to think that … but now …

I used to feel strongly about … but now …

I used to always … but now …

I used to never … but now …

NOTICING THE UNCHANGING

Let come what comes, let go what goes.
See what remains.

– RAMANA MAHARSHI

E ven after all these years, I still find myself drawn to the mystery of who I am, to the beauty and the miracle of life. I still find myself drawn to the wonders of the universe and human nature. I am still fascinated by the power of writing to teach me empathy, kindness, and truth. Writing has never stopped being my compass for compassion and self-honesty, my mirror and my poetry. It's like a night sky full of possibilities and mystery, and I still give myself to it fully each day. Even after all these years, I still find the same love in my heart for everyone I've ever loved, even if they may no longer be in my life. I still feel indebted to life for everything it offers me. I'm still amazed by the miracles each day brings. I'm grateful.

Even though change is constant, there are some things inside us that remain unchanged. They may be our core beliefs. A sense of our true essence. They can also be the most stubborn parts of us. You are the only one who knows the difference among these. You might be drawn to the same things you loved when you were a kid. You might also be falling into the same trap that you did ten years ago.

You won't know what hasn't changed unless you look. Otherwise, an old trajectory that you never revised might lead you in a direction you might not want to go.

Take a good look at what has never changed in your life. You can start with, "Even after all these years, I still find myself …" and follow your mind wherever it takes you for seven minutes.

CHOOSING A DIRECTION

If you do not change direction, you may end
up where you are heading.

– LAO TZU

Change is the only permanent thing in life. Sometimes it occurs naturally and spontaneously. Other times we resist it because entering the unknown often feels scary and unsafe. But imagining the changes that would make us happier is a safe place to start from. Before you have to make any actual changes, you can use the magic of writing to try them out. No harm done, and a greater clarity is likely to come in just a few minutes.

Think of three things you would like to change in your life right now. There might be a thousand changes you want to make all at once, but for now, try to focus on the three most important and most pressing ones. They can be physical, metaphysical, social, familial, financial, psychological, emotional, spiritual, etc. They can be tiny or monumental, realistic or fantastic—but they have to be important to you right now. You can start with, "The three things I would change in my life right now are ..." and freewrite for seven minutes.

MOVING WITH THE SEASONS

Sometimes all it takes to change a life is to decide which beliefs do not serve you and to literally change your mind about those beliefs.

– JOY PAGE

When it comes to our self-image, each of us carries around many old beliefs. You may have received them as gifts from your well-meaning parents. They might have generously gifted you with, "You are too slow, too clumsy, too timid, too proud, too small, too stupid, too smart, too much of a tomboy, too girly, etc." Any one of these beliefs doesn't carry too much weight, but when you put them all together, they begin to weigh you down without your noticing. Some of them might have become too tight and restrictive for you now, like clothes you have outgrown. Most importantly, they are not consciously yours. You might not even remember how you got them, or who gave them to you, but it doesn't matter because you don't have to keep them after today.

It's time for some spring cleaning. You are no longer the child who had to accept these beliefs. You can redefine yourself, so you no longer need any hand-me-downs. Open all the windows, let the fresh air in, let the curtains fly, take all of your old "clothes" out of your closet, and try on each one of them. Do they still fit, or is it time to let them go? Are you still clumsy? Are you still slow? Examine one belief at a time and design a whole new wardrobe consisting of things that fit you now and that you can wear with pride. Find at least ten pieces that fit you comfortably right now. You can also include those pieces that don't fit yet, but hopefully will do so with a little bit of practice. Here's my current capsule wardrobe:

I am strong.

I am kind.

I am creative.

I am compassionate.

I am thoughtful.

I am trusting.

I am open.

I am capable of change.

I am empathetic.

I embrace my femininity.

Now freewrite for seven minutes about how you feel about this wardrobe change and what it feels like to wear these new beliefs.

CHOOSING BETWEEN ADVENTURE AND SECURITY

The price of anything is the amount of life
you exchange for it.

– HENRY DAVID THOREAU

Part of us loves change and adventure, and part of us prefers safety and security. Since we were kids, we were taught that it's better to be safe than sorry, but our adventurous side is still alive in us and wants a chance to express itself once in a while. There isn't one aspect of ourselves that's better than the other, but far too often we stick to listening to just one of those voices. If you have ever regretted not doing or saying something, not taking action, and not taking a risk, then you know that being safe is not always better than being sorry.

Imagine yourself in the future, at a crucial moment in your life when you are facing an important decision and struggling to make a choice. You are about to make a big change in your life. Write to your future self in order to encourage and empower yourself. Write a letter to that part of yourself that is not afraid to take risks or explore new possibilities. Let them know how proud you are of them for taking a risk and valuing freedom and a sense of discovery. Notice what it feels like to communicate with that part of yourself. What can it give you, and what can you learn from it? What does it feel like to get in touch with that side of yourself?

Now write a paragraph on behalf of the part of yourself that needs to feel safe and secure. What does it want to say to you? What does it want to caution you about? Do you share its fears? You can even write a dialogue between these two parts.

SENSING THE SHAPE
OF TRANSITIONS

Life is one big transition.

– WILLIE STARGELL

We are always becoming. Never stagnant. Our bodies are changing, and so are our feelings and our moods, our frame of mind and worldview. We never simply are, but we are constantly becoming. The present moment connects your past and your future. It is a dynamic transition from your past self to your future self. You may be transitioning between relationships, jobs, places, hobbies, schools. You may have left a familiar shore and can't see the other one just yet.

Usually, we are rushing through this moment unaware of its shape, unaware of the transformation that is taking place because we are preparing to meet our future goals and focusing on our future tasks. So, a meaningful transformation may go by unnoticed. Writing can allow you a brief moment of awareness when you can notice the transformation and pay attention to its shape and direction.

Right now, feel into the nature of the current transition in your life. What does it feel and look like? Where are you right now? Where is your soul going? Whom are you becoming? Try to intuit the answers and write about the direction you're being pulled in right now.

Find a helpful image, a metaphor that can symbolize what the transformation feels like, or what you would like the transformation to be. Are you changing from a caterpillar into a butterfly, from a frog into a princess, from a scared child into a superhero? Find an image that speaks to you and freewrite to explore it. You can start by saying, "Right now I feel like ..." and write for seven minutes.

CHAPTER 10

RELATIONSHIP
WITH SPACE

CREATING A PERFECT
WRITING PLACE

I have my favorite cat, who is my
paperweight, on my desk while I am writing.

– RAY BRADBURY

When I'm in my perfect writing place, I hear the sounds of water. Whether it's the beach, a riverbank, or the little waterfall in our courtyard. I see the sun peeking through the trees while I'm safely tucked away in the shade of a giant maple tree. Its bark feels both sensual and supportive against my back. I feel a caress of breeze on my skin. I feel light, without a care in the world. The water, the sun, the shade, the breeze, and the trunk's support help my writing blossom.

I love writing through the moment. I feel perfectly complete, and I let the bird song and the rustling of the leaves guide me on my writing journey. They're here, and I'm here, and we're not different—the rustling of the leaves and the rhythm of my

170

breath. I listen to them speak and read my thoughts as they turn the pages. I hear their truth, their kindness, and I speak mine. Love is here in my writing to awaken me to its truth, and I'm feeling blessed by it.

Having a perfect writing place is terribly important. Writing places can inspire you and infuse your writing with their energy. Even if you don't get to visit your perfect writing place physically as often as you'd like, you can always go there in your imagination. Chances are you have experienced or at least imagined a writing place that makes you happy. But have you taken time to notice what is it exactly in our surroundings that nourishes or inhibits your creativity?

Today create a perfect writing place for yourself. A sacred space to hold your thoughts and intentions, feelings and emotions, sorrows and regrets, doubts and decisions. A place that can hold your whole self. To begin, imagine yourself any place you would like, and surround yourself with anything you want there. You could choose to sit under a tree, on top of one, on the rocks, on the chair, on the carpet or on the grass. Or you could sit underwater, ride a cloud, sit by the fire, alone or with friends who are also writing. You could sit on a shore, stare at the horizon, or get carried away by the waves.

Surround yourself with anything that could give your writing some energy and a creative boost. Are you inside or outside? In nature or in a busy café? You can design a season, a weather, and time of day. Are you alone? Are there others writing, walking, or playing nearby? You can have the whole park to yourself, or be surrounded by people or animals you like. Do you smell coffee or freshly baked bread? Do you hear a waterfall or the sound of crashing waves? What do you feel like when you are there? Describe your perfect writing place in detail for seven minutes. You can begin with, "When I'm in my perfect writing place … "

ENJOYING A DIVERSION PERMIT

*We are so obsessed with doing that we have
no time and no imagination left for being.
As a result, men are valued not for what they
are but for what they do or what they have—
for their usefulness.*

– THOMAS MERTON

In North American culture, we are used to straight lines.
The city streets are straight, the buildings and their
hallways are, for the most part, straight. We walk in straight
lines, from point A to point B, without letting ourselves stop
and take a detour if we notice something interesting. Without
taking a pause to stand and appreciate the scenery or walk
around a park, just for the fun of it. There's rarely a curved
path among the trees to walk leisurely on, or a labyrinth
for contemplative reflective circling. Meandering or walking

without a destination is not a huge part of our cultural conditioning. Often, it is frowned upon.

No wonder we are used to thinking in straight lines as well. How can I get from now (point A) to my goal (point B) as fast as possible, without detours and without wasting time? We think of ourselves as being on a specific career path, and we expect our life journey to unfold in a straight line. Our goals are laid out and yet, sometimes, we find ourselves dreaming about other paths worth exploring—paths not taken and paths still possible. We have all skipped class to explore the unknown—one of the sweet forbidden luxuries of childhood, when we could still hear our spirit talk to us and demand freedom.

If you could allow yourself three small diversions today, what would they be? Inviting a friend to take a walk in the middle of your workday? Catching snowflakes with your tongue for ten seconds? Calling an old friend, or better yet, showing up on their doorstep with a cake or a bottle of wine and announcing proudly that you've come to visit for no reason at all? Maybe just cloud watching for fifteen minutes? Could you allow your soul the luxury of stepping out of your daily routine and indulging in what it needs in this moment? You can start with, "If I allowed myself three diversions today, I would ..." and go on for seven minutes before you continue with the next prompt.

If life were to give you a permission slip for one magical diversion this year with absolutely no consequences, what would you do with it? Where would you go and with whom? Climb Mount Everest? Hike down the Grand Canyon? Take a silent retreat? Pull your kids from school for a year and go travelling around the world? Take time out of your life to help a neighbour build a deck just for the fun of it, while expecting nothing in return? What diversion does your soul want right now? You can begin with, "If I allowed myself one big diversion this year, I would …" and freewrite for seven minutes.

SEARCHING FOR HOME

The ache for home lives in all of us, the safe place where we can go as we are and not be questioned.

– MAYA ANGELOU

Home is a place we all need. Most of the time, we take our home for granted, but millions of people will never get to enjoy this luxury. They have no place to go when the night falls. My own family have been displaced for over five years. War came unannounced. And in one split second, both peace and home were gone. Home is a place that can give us a sense of safety, peace, love, and acceptance. It's a place where it's safe to be ourselves and put our worries and our pain down for just a little bit. Home gives us hope and energy, a place to rest and restore.

We often slip into a rut and go about our days without noticing our relationship with our home. Without feeling into whether it supports us or drains us of our energy. Today, take a closer look. Explore what it means to you to feel at home. Quickly answer the questions below and freewrite about any of them whenever there's more to explore.

Does your current home feel like home? Why or why not?

What needs of yours are fulfilled by having a home?

Which part of your home do you feel happiest in? Is it your bed, your favourite chair by the window, your desk, or your writing studio? Or maybe a spot on the floor because there's so much room around you to spread out anything you need?

If your home were a colour, what colour would it be and why?

If you could throw away all the clutter and keep only five things, what would they be?

What do you like to feel when you come home after a long day of work?

What three things would you love to change about your home right now?

What three things do you love the most about your home and would never change?

Is there a place outside your home that feels like home? What makes it feel like home?

EXPLORING HOMELESSNESS

We think sometimes that poverty is only being hungry, naked and homeless. The poverty of being unwanted, unloved and uncared for is the greatest poverty. We must start in our own homes to remedy this kind of poverty.

– MOTHER TERESA

Our hearts are large enough to experience both sides of anything. So now that we have explored our feelings about home, we can take courage to explore our feelings about homelessness, especially if they make us uncomfortable. What would it feel like not to have a home? Usually, we would try to avoid feeling into this idea, but we don't have to be afraid of temporary discomfort. It often comes with a great opportunity to learn something valuable.

Tap into the feelings that surface when you meet a homeless person in the street. What feeling is the first one to stir up in you? Is it a feeling of compassion, awkwardness, embarrassment, fear, discomfort? Try to be as specific as possible and start with, "Sometimes, when I see a homeless person, I feel ..." Write for seven minutes and gather specific feelings that you are normally afraid to feel and acknowledge.

Now turn your attention inwards. Is there a part of you that has been homeless for a while? Which part of you doesn't have a home? What is it that you're not letting in? Do you need to hide your imperfections? Do you keep your fears out of the house? Have you changed the lock on your heart when some old familiar pain showed up at your door and asked to come in? What doesn't have a home in the space of your heart and has to stay out at all times? You can start by writing, "One part of me that still hasn't found a home in my heart is ..." and continue for seven minutes.

FINDING A NEW PERSPECTIVE

One's destination is never a place but rather
a new way of looking at things.

– HENRY MILLER

Sometimes, our life feels too crowded. We're restricted by our thoughts and beliefs, overwhelmed by what's happening around us and the never-ending distractions. We are full of ideas, problems, solutions. We are tense and tight. To others, we might appear tense and closed off as well. People will intuitively feel there's no space in us to welcome them when they meet us. We urgently need some space. Lots of it. And we need some air. Having a little bit of distance from our life, our tasks, and problems is likely to give us a fresh, unexpected perspective on how to approach things with more wisdom and more space in our thoughts and actions. Writing is a teleportation device that can take us to such imaginary place that offers a lot of openness and space.

Create an image in your mind that has a lot of space and a clear view of the horizon. Transport yourself there. It might be a beach, the top of a mountain, or the roof of a skyscraper offering a view of the sky and the stars. Now that you are in that space, invite any of your latest problems to show up— preferably, a problem that's been with you for the last little while. Ask it to take shape in front of you. Give it a seat of honour and invite it to speak freely about all its fears. Listen. Feel into your relationship with this problem without losing perspective on the place you're in. Once in a while, shift your gaze from the problem to the space around it and feel the openness of this space. Keep shifting your gaze back and forth to see if it's still talking, trying to evoke a reaction in you, or if it got quiet and appears different. Maybe it's even fading out and appears more like a hologram. Keep your gaze on the open space around you while listening to the voice of your problem.

Write about your experience. Start by describing the space where you are and how the problem appeared when it showed up first. Write about how you felt when it started to speak, and what it said. For seven minutes, keep reflecting on your feelings and note any shifts in your perspective.

181

CREATING A SAFE PLACE

Music was my refuge. I could crawl into the
space between the notes and curl my back to
loneliness.

– MAYA ANGELOU

When I'm in my safe place, the world stops. Time stands still. I'm not running anywhere. I'm in complete serenity. Here, I am free of thought, empty and floating above ground. I am light, spacious, beautiful, empty, and silent. I am just here, blown around by the wind. I am free to be and to feel everything. I am here to be what I am instead of imagining. Love is here to teach me everything I already know. There's wisdom arising from the silence inside. There's beauty. There's peace. There's fullness and love in my heart.

All of us need a safe place. A beautiful and healing place. A sacred one. A place where we can be free. A place where we can hide from the world for a while as deep reflection or deep healing takes place. Do you have one? It doesn't have to

182

be real. Imagination can take you places just as well. It doesn't have to be a physical place either. It is very easy to find a safe haven by getting lost in a book, in music, in writing, or in a work of art. Your safe place can even be a person.

Write about your safe place where you come to hide and to heal when the world becomes too much to handle. You might have more than one safe place, but for now, write about one of them. Where do you go? What is the magic of this place? How does it help you heal? What transformation takes place? Freewrite for seven minutes.

CHAPTER 11

RELATIONSHIP
WITH FREEDOM

UNLOCKING

Why do you stay in prison when the door is
so wide open?

– RUMI

We all create prisons. By choice—even though we rarely think so. We feel restricted and locked in and don't know whom to blame for it. Who locked us in? It may seem that the prison was imposed by some external circumstances. And sometimes it is indeed external circumstances restricting us, but often it's none other than our own mind and our undiscovered internal beliefs.

Writing allows us a chance to identify all the prisons we've locked ourselves in. And if we pay close attention, we might be lucky enough to find the key that unlocks our cell.

Imagine yourself stuck behind bars. Write down who or what you feel is responsible for your feeling of unfreedom. What keeps you feeling locked in? Is it your job, your career, your house, your culture, your marriage? What's holding you back? Try to identify which thoughts, feelings, and beliefs are preventing you from opening the door to your freedom and leaving the prison behind. Freewrite for seven minutes.

Look outside. What do you see beyond the bars? What's pulling you to leave the prison and meet a world of new possibilities? Freewrite for seven minutes about the things you are dying to do, start, or revisit.

Now imagine one possible way to leave your prison and step into freedom. If it helps, think about a role model who has done what you want to do. You can freewrite about how they accomplished it. What do you admire about them the most? What was calling them to step outside, and what was keeping them from leaving their cell in the first place? Where did they find the strength to move towards freedom? What was the key that unlocked their prison cell, and can you use the same key to unlock yours? Freewrite for seven minutes.

WRITING TO FIND FREEDOM

*Mind is consciousness which has put on
limitations. You are originally unlimited and
perfect. Later you take on limitations and
become the mind.*

– RAMANA MAHARSHI

Freedom. We all want it. We talk about it, dream about it, and some of us even die for it. It is elusive. Everyone knows about it, but no one knows where it's hiding. We are all blessed with life and freedom. We are free, yet we often feel bound. I wonder why we feel that. I also wonder whether we are using this feeling of unfreedom as an excuse to keep from doing something we say we want. What do we want the freedom for? Often, we talk about wanting to do ten things, but given a free afternoon, we invent excuses to stay on the sofa. Sounds just a little suspicious, doesn't it?

We are always free to be ourselves, and to be more than just our little self. We are free to be ourselves fully right now, even

188

with all of our little imperfections. Not when we lose weight, get that job, grow taller, richer, or finish that degree. Nothing is excluded from freedom. Everything is welcome in this space of freedom on the page.

Take a moment to explore your relationship with freedom. What freedoms are you craving? What freedoms are missing from your life? What freedoms would you like to give yourself today? Take a minute or so to make a quick list. For example:

The freedom to make decisions

The freedom to play

The freedom to pursue my interests

The freedom to express myself

The freedom to create something true, beautiful, and unique

The freedom to make time for myself

After you make your list, freewrite for seven minutes reflecting on any one freedom from your list. Notice any thoughts or feelings you experienced when writing the list.

BREAKING FREE FROM YOUR MIND

Yesterday I was clever, so I wanted to change the world. Today I am wise, so I am changing myself.

– RUMI

One of the most common prisons we build for ourselves is in our mind. And one of the most common ways we lock ourselves in is by committing to a set of unrealistic rules and standards that we impose on ourselves. Upholding these takes a lot of effort. It brings about stress and drains us of energy. Nothing about them is true, and if we believe them, they hold us prisoner. Instead of meeting life as it is, we insist that life goes according to our expectations.

What do you secretly expect of yourself? Take a moment to list your unhelpful rules, standards, and expectations for yourself. For example:

I should be better or at least as good as others.

I don't belong here.

I must be perfect all the time.

I can't make any mistakes.

There is no room for error.

I must not fail.

If I make a mistake, it will be catastrophic.

I can't have others think negatively of me.

I will disappoint others.

After you list them, reflect on each of them and rewrite it to be more flexible, realistic, useful, and compassionate.

PLANNING A SECRET ESCAPE

Every person needs to take one day away.
A day in which one consciously separates the
past from the future. Jobs, family, employers,
and friends can exist one day without any one
of us, and if our egos permit us to confess,
they could exist eternally in our absence. Each
person deserves a day away in which no
problems are confronted, no solutions searched
for. Each of us needs to withdraw from the
cares which will not withdraw from us.

– MAYA ANGELOU

We all have days when we want to get away from it all. As the pressure of expectations builds, we're desperately searching for a pause button so that we can put the world on hold and get out. So that—even if only for fifteen minutes— we can take a little break from our life. Life can get tough, overwhelming, too fast, or too demanding. The more we feel restricted by circumstances, the more we want to take off the chains and disappear.

That's when on the spur of the moment, we feel dangerously close to making a sudden move, like quitting our job or moving across the world. We are ready to make a radical change, which comes with a lot of radical consequences. Writing can give us a chance to do precisely that but with zero consequences. It can give us the desired break from reality and allow us to sneak away for an hour or two and get lost in our imagination.

Imagine that for the next three hours, you can escape anywhere in the world without worrying about any logistics, like time, money, or flight schedules. Right now, you are not limited by anything but your imagination. You can even go to the past or the future. No packing, no planning, and definitely no flying. Just an ordinary teleportation through the magic of writing.

Freewrite about a three-hour escape you would take today. Where would you go if you could leave right now? What would you do? Whom would you visit? What would you say or give to them? Freewrite for seven minutes.

WRITING THROUGH ADDICTION

Every form of addiction is bad, no matter
whether the narcotic be alcohol or morphine
or idealism.

– CARL JUNG

We are all addicted to something, but I doubt we would freely admit it. Our addictions don't have to be such common culprits as drugs or alcohol. We can be addicted to looking perfect, watching TV for hours, daily gossip, being right, or arguing with our spouse. We can be addicted to knitting, eating, running, sex, social media, cleaning—anything really. These activities are not harmful in and of themselves, but the obsessive quality we bring to them makes them take over our lives in a sneaky way.

Take an honest look at yourself. Make a list of things you are addicted to. It might be hard to do, but you deserve to know and understand yourself and your choices. If it doesn't feel comfortable to name them, use code or abbreviations, or just call them something else, like an orange. Explore why you love each of these things so much. What draws you to them? What feeling or change in mood does it give you? How do you feel after you got your fix? Does it feel like you've had enough? Is it ever enough? What thoughts are going through your mind as you're exploring this difficult topic? Collect them without judgment—they will give you powerful insights.

WRITING TO GET UNSTUCK

Your life is unfolding naturally. Leave it be!
It does not need any help.

– MOOJI

If I look honestly at all the times I felt stuck, frustrated, or anxious, I can always find certain expectations I had about the way things had to be in order for me to be happy. If we have no expectations of the present moment, then life is free to go any way it pleases, and we simply flow with it. If we refuse to accept things as they are, we will feel stuck. Guaranteed. Even if we want to change things, acting from a place of frustration is rarely productive.

We must start from the place of complete acceptance of the present moment. Then our actions will be clear and powerful. If you cannot accept what is going on right now, you are stuck in a hopeless battle with reality. There's nothing wrong with fighting reality—we've all tried it. The trouble is life will go on the way it will. You can find wisdom and strength in accepting life fully, being humbled by its mystery and grateful for it. Being in the place of acceptance can save you a lot of energy, leaving space for clear decisions and actions. Resistance, on the other hand, would drain you of vital energy, leaving you exhausted and depleted.

Identifying expectations is not easy. But when they are seen, you can judge how helpful they are. Often, the simple act of writing them down reveals their untruth, and they fall away by themselves. Think of a situation where you feel stuck. Reflect on what frustrates you the most about it, and how you would like for it to be resolved. What part of your self-image would such resolution serve? Can you identify your expectations the moment you became frustrated? What was your desired outcome? What feeling would it have given you? What did you have to feel instead? Freewrite for seven minutes to discover your hidden expectations. Don't judge yourself as you're discovering them.

Instead of getting frustrated about the difference between your expectations and reality, try asking, "What can I appreciate in this situation right now?" and freewrite for seven minutes. And even if you cannot discover anything to appreciate right away, at least you have tried. And in doing this, you might have taken the most important step of setting the intention to look for things to appreciate instead of judge. Life tends to notice things like that.

TESTING OUTER LIMITS

Everything comes to us that belongs to us if
we create the capacity to receive it.
– RABINDRANATH TAGORE

Whether consciously or unconsciously, all of us define ourselves and our life. We draw invisible lines around us to distinguish ourselves from others. We also draw lines around life that only exist in our imagination, thus limiting life in its ability to surprise us. As we become adults, we already know too much about the way things work, which in turn excludes the possibility of miracles. We have already learned all about definitions and boundaries. Thank goodness that life ignores the boundaries and limitations we invented and amazes us still. We call these moments miracles.

What are some parts of your life where you feel limited? Where would you like more freedom and space? What would it take for you to feel more freedom in your life? Whom could you ask for your freedom and power? Who keeps them hostage? What could you rearrange to feel freer? Can you identify the external boundaries you perceive?

What about internal ones? Start with this moment. What have you imposed on it? What beliefs, rules, standards, or expectations can you see through? What would help you feel freer and more inspired? Can you think of three imagined limitations that no longer serve you? What are some unhelpful thoughts that weigh heavily on you? Why are they in your mind space? What gifts are you not ready to receive? What gifts are you ready to receive? Freewrite for seven minutes.

CHAPTER 12

RELATIONSHIP
WITH ATTENTION

WRITING TO NOTICE

There is more to life than increasing its speed.

– MAHATMA GANDHI

Is it just me, or the older you get, the faster life speeds by? When we take life for granted, it becomes easy to miss the most delicious parts of each day. Things that make our life a bit richer and more inspired are often the simplest ones.

Every year, I look forward to the freshness of the new season. The first snow, the budding of the trees, the rain, the warmth of the sun on my face, sitting on Ward's Island with my ankles buried in the sand.

Each day, I look forward to walking home from work. I look forward to stopping at the park just to sit purposelessly on a bench and dangle my feet while watching birds, dogs, flowers, and kids weave a perfect life fabric. Each moment is unique. It's so easy to lose track of time watching puppies chase squirrels, cloud watching, or staring at the church steeple and listening to the chiming of the bells. I look forward to coming home to my husband and sharing our day with each other, with words or without. I look forward to passing by my favourite florist's shop and taking in the beauty of his art. If he's not busy, I usually say hello and stop for a brief chat. I look forward to climbing the hill in front of my house before sunset and staying there until the world's two mysterious forces meet—the light and the darkness.

Take a closer look at your day and make a list of twenty-five things you love having in your day. Take a few minutes to appreciate them. Write down whatever comes to mind. This is not the final list, and you are not going to laminate it or share it with anyone, so there's no need to worry when putting it together. After the list is complete, freewrite about one or two of the items that spoke to you the most. You don't have to stop at twenty-five either. This can be your running appreciation list, and you could practice noticing and adding a few new items each day.

WRITING TO WANDER

Writing is an exploration. You start from nothing and learn as you go.

— E. L. DOCTOROW

Writing is a lot like wandering. Writing allows us to wander aimlessly in our mind and notice our thoughts. Writing doesn't ask anything of us. We are not required to get anywhere. In fact, if anything, we are asked to remain here in the present moment and follow our pen and our thoughts wherever they take us. And if we want to turn right, we are free to do so. And if we feel like switching directions for no reason at all, writing will not ask us for a reason—it never does. It allows anything without hesitation. It offers space to anything and receives our wandering with love.

Every time you write, you are touching and exploring a different part of yourself by bringing your soul to the page. Writing allows you to take a new path, find a new path, make a new path, find a new sound, maybe even create a new song.

You can see each moment anew, from a new place inside. Same life. Different perspective.

Every time you come to the blank page, you can breathe in freedom. You can touch the blank space of the page and remember your Self. You can travel to places unknown, inhale beauty and freedom, and stay as the blank page that life itself writes on.

Today, release any expectations of your writing, and let it lead the way. Follow with trust wherever it takes you. Allow yourself to wander aimlessly in your thoughts and feelings. The truth is you cannot write around yourself, so wherever you start, what is important to you will manifest on the page. But for this to happen, you must trust writing more than you trust yourself.

Take a pen and write the first thing that comes to mind. You can start with, "If I allow myself to wander aimlessly right now, the first thing I feel is …" and continue without any goal or purpose for seven minutes. Do not reread right away. You can come back to it in a couple of days to take a fresh look.

USING THE POWER OF LISTS

*I don't try to guess what a million people will
like. It's hard enough to know what I like.*

– JOHN HUSTON

Lists are deceivingly simple, but their power is underestimated. They are a wonderful tool for quickly taking down your thoughts and feelings before the mind has a chance to resist or comment. Lists can be a source of powerful insights into your life. They can surprise you and encourage you to take action. The most important part is to write them in a spontaneous and playful way. Try this very simple exercise right now.

Take a few minutes just to pay attention to what you like and don't like. Start by making a list of three colours you like; then add three books and three foods you love; three places you've been to that you love; and three activities you enjoy.

Now, make another list of three colours that don't appeal to you: three foods you can't stomach; three books you couldn't finish; three places you hope to never return to; and finally, three activities you cannot stand.

Reflect on what you've written. What does each list make you feel? What memories or emotions do you associate with these places, books, foods, activities, and colours? Freewrite about both lists for seven minutes.

OPENLY WATCHING

Give yourself a gift of five minutes of contemplation in awe of everything you see around you. Go outside and turn your attention to the many miracles around you. This five-minute-a-day regimen of appreciation and gratitude will help you to focus your life in awe.

— WAYNE DYER

What is the meaning of life? What is its purpose? What does it feel like to be alive? What is life? How often do you stop to feel into the miracle of life and be crushed and awestruck by it? Most of us waste a lot of precious moments worrying about details. We often take life's simplicity and superimpose our heavy mental structures on it. Then we wonder why we are so drained and lifeless at the end of the day. We spend our energy unwisely. We miss the miracle, the beauty, and the fullness of each moment.

Wherever you find yourself right now, for the next five minutes, do not focus your attention on anything specific, and simply watch the movement of life with openness and curiosity. Notice what's going on around you. Connect with the feelings of gratitude and wonder at the orchestration of it all. No thoughts can stay for too long in the light of gratitude and wonder. Try feeling fully into this moment in your life, the miracle of all other people who have blessed your life with their presence. Notice life in the animals, trees, and plants around you. Notice life itself. Can you see the simple movement of life in everything around you?

Notice what's going on inside you. In the same way, no thoughts, no interpretations or conclusions. Just notice the sense of being alive. Isn't it enough to be alive, to feel it all and take it all in? Try to be empty of any ideas about life, and just watch the show that life has put on for you. After you've sat openly with what's going on outside and inside you for about five minutes, freewrite about your experience using unfocused attention for seven more minutes, bringing awareness to any feelings or insights.

FINDING A FOCUS

Simplicity is the ultimate sophistication.

– LEONARDO DA VINCI

Our lives are full. They are filled to the brim with important things, tasks, people, activities, and events. This is wonderful and can make us feel fulfilled and, well, important— but it can also easily become distracting. We fill our days with dozens of chores, we fill our lists with hundreds of tasks, and we rush from one important thing to another all day. And in the midst of it all, we might miss some of the things in life that truly are important, in the fullest sense of the word. In order to change this, I'm inviting you to play a simple game.

Adjust the focus lens of your perception and select the most important aspect of your life right now. What is one thing that is important to you today? Only one. Write it down.

After writing it down, pick one focus for this week. What is it? Continue writing about only one pertinent thing you'd like to focus on this month; then another one for this year; and only one for your entire life. Take some time to simplify your life on paper. If two things come to mind, write them both down, then feel which one seems more important and cross the other one out. This is called "The Focusing Game" for a reason.

Using your intuition, keep writing until a clear focus emerges, and three important items become two, and then only one. Write until you feel at peace with the focus you've selected. Don't worry about choosing only one thing—you are not committing to it for life. In fact, you don't have to do anything about it. Simply imagine it and write it down. This is just a silly game—that's all. Allow the results to surprise you.

WRITING FOR CLARITY

Put your ear down close to your soul and
listen hard.

— ANNE SEXTON

I'd live for years without stopping to notice what was important to me at any given moment. I often felt like I was constantly on call to help others with their priorities. Isn't this what nice people do? No. This is not nice. It's not nice at all if I forget to stop and ask myself what's important to me. Journaling has completely changed this habit. I find that staying connected with things that are important to me, even if I can't get to them today, tomorrow, or this week, helps me stay clear about my life. Just to have this conversation with myself opens a new dimension of clarity in my relationship with my own life. It's worth spending fifteen minutes a day, or even a week, on clearing my life of mental debris so I can see the true path unfold before me.

It would be a shame to miss your own journey. What is important to you right now? Take a moment to write down ten different areas of your life—for example, spiritual, emotional, physical, relational, career, etc. It doesn't have to be any of these examples if they don't resonate with you. In each category, write down one goal that is important to you right now. Try to remember what was important to you a year or five years ago in each category. Write that down as well. What have you noticed about your current list and the one from your past? Are there any similarities? What about the differences? Reflect on both lists for seven minutes.

RECONNECTING WITH PEACE

Better than a thousand hollow words, is one
word that brings peace.

– BUDDHA

Everything around us has a specific and, often, distinct energy. In that way, what surrounds us can affect our own energy and our sense of wellbeing. It's as if both the inner and outer space interact and eventually align with each other. We have all experienced people and places that bring peace into our lives. Some places are naturally cozy, some activities are naturally soothing, and some people are naturally gentle, and their presence feels comforting. They have a certain peaceful energy about them that is clearly felt but perhaps hard to pinpoint.

We don't usually stop to notice this, but it might be helpful to discover which people, places, and activities bring us a feeling of peace and harmony, and which ones don't. You might be able to cultivate these feelings of peace and harmony by consciously looking for ways to spend time with people who bring peace into your life, visit places that have a peaceful energy, and engage in activities that bring you to a place of peace.

Start by dividing the page into two columns. In the first one, list all the people, places, activities, and experiences that bring you a feeling of peace. In the second one, list those that don't. Freewrite about anything or anyone in the first column. Notice the unique ways they contribute to your peace. You can start with, "I feel most peaceful when ..." and write non-stop for seven minutes.

CHAPTER 13

RELATIONSHIP
WITH MAGIC

BECOMING A SUPERHERO

If you want happiness for an hour, take a nap.
If you want happiness for a day, go fishing.
If you want happiness for a month, get married.
If you want happiness for a year, inherit a fortune.
If you want happiness for a lifetime, help
somebody else.

– CHINESE PROVERB

We all love superheroes. We love what they stand for and envy their superpowers. We want to be just like them—to be able to fly, breathe underwater, read minds, time travel, and most importantly, help others. We want to be larger than life and stand for justice, kindness, and truth. We are used to thinking that superpowers belong only to superheroes, but this is not necessarily true. Writing can give us any superpower we can dream of.

What superpower would you love to have? Describe it in detail. Freewrite about how you could use it to help someone. Whom would you help and why? You can choose someone you know or someone you don't know—a friend, a family member, a homeless person at the corner of your street, someone you read about on the news, a colleague who seems a little sad lately, a neighbour. Anyone really. It doesn't even have to be one person. You can choose to help a group of people, a family, a country, our planet. There are no limits to using your life to serve something larger than yourself. You can start by writing, "If I had a superpower, I would ..." and freewrite for seven minutes.

INVENTING AN ENCHANTED OBJECT

Logic will get you from A to B. Imagination
will take you everywhere.

– ALBERT EINSTEIN

Have you ever been in a situation where no matter how many solutions you've tried, nothing is working, so you end up feeling stuck and desperate? I have been in plenty of such situations, where I officially ran out of moves. I would try figuring it out for myself, doing research, and turning to family and friends for advice. When that didn't work, I would just wish for some magical solution to appear out of the blue. Writing allows us to design our own magical inventions that could help us navigate any situation that we feel is difficult to handle.

Think of an enchanted object that you could use in your life right now. Invent an object that would provide a magical solution to situations you find difficult or unpleasant. What is your invention, and what are its powers? How could you use it in your life right now? Whom would it affect and how, and is anyone immune to its magic?

After you have used this enchanted object in your own life, you can share it with someone else. Whom would you share it with and why? What can it do for them? What are they going through? What quality, understanding, or strength are they missing? What would you like your object to give them? You can start with, "I really wish I had a ..." and freewrite for seven minutes.

LOADING A MAGICAL VENDING MACHINE

This world is but a canvas to our imagination.

— HENRY DAVID THOREAU

We all go through challenging times where we could use a little pick-me-up. Things may not have gone as planned, or someone may have said something careless or hurtful. There are many circumstances that would bring us down in an instant. Our automatic response might be to get upset, angry, or sad, but after our initial reaction subsides, we could always try something new to help us avoid getting stuck in a loop of emotions. Something that would help us return to our normal selves fairly quickly.

Imagine that you can pre-load a magical vending machine with some of your favourite moments that you can retrieve later when you are not feeling so great. Take a few minutes to recall some of your favourite experiences. I'm talking about those that fill you with joy and melt your face into one big grin, no matter what you are doing. Try recalling as many special memories as you can. They may range from watching a sunset from the top of a hill, to your first kiss, to sitting on your favourite beach and building a sandcastle, to having your favourite ice-cream flavour on a hot summer day. Any memory that you'd like to savour goes into the vending machine. Pre-load at least ten small precious memory tokens that you can use later as a pick-me-up. It works!

REVIVING A MAGICAL
DIMENSION OF LIFE

The world is full of magical things patiently
waiting for our wits to grow sharper.

– BERTRAND RUSSELL

All of us are attracted to mystery. We are drawn to magic and miracles. In fact, when we were little, life was naturally filled with a sense of wonder. There were fairies in the garden, witches in the dark attic, Santa on the roof, and gnomes hiding in the trees. The wind was singing songs we could understand, and we all had a magical place we could go to in reality or our imagination.

Do you remember what was filled with magic when you were a kid? Where did it go? What replaced your belief in magic? Some of us kept that belief in the magical nature of the universe, and some of us lost it. What about you?

224

Explore your relationship with the magical dimension of life by reflecting on the questions below:

Is any part of your life open to magic? Which part?

What is the place of magic in your life?

Do you believe that life is large enough to allow for magic and miracles? Did you use to?

When did your belief in magic change? Do you remember the precise moment?

Which new beliefs replaced it?

You can start by writing, "When I was a kid, I used to believe that ..." and continue for seven minutes.

COLLECTING WISHES

Is freedom anything else than the right to live
as we wish? Nothing else.

– EPICTETUS

The ability to dream is terribly important. Even more so is the ability to dream big and often. We usually live our days drowning in obstacles and challenges, crises and limitations. We are used to being in a rut and focusing on our negative circumstances or limitations. It rarely occurs to us to approach this moment as an ever-open portal into what's possible. I feel that setting aside a regular time and taking that time to dream and wish upon a star is like yoga for our imagination muscles. The more we practice and stretch, the more flexible our imagination can become.

Give yourself the gift of freedom and write down twenty wishes. They don't have to be grand. Twenty is a large enough number to include all kinds of wishes, so no pressure. You can start with the most trivial ones, like "I wish my hair was long enough to make a ponytail," and keep collecting your wishes big and small. Write until you have nothing else to wish for. Try not to push. Take time to listen. To help you trick your mind into completing the list, start by writing down numbers from one to twenty. You can keep writing past twenty if you feel there are more wishes to be collected. After you've finished your list, freewrite for seven minutes about some of the wishes that stood out and feel alive with energy.

CREATING A WORLD
OF YOUR OWN

After one look at this planet any visitor from
outer space would say 'I want to see the
manager.'

– WILLIAM S. BURROUGHS

At one time or another, we all felt restricted by circumstances. Whether it's our job, people around us, the weather, the politics, the climate, you name it, there were moments when we wished we could change our reality. It's hard to do in real life, but in writing, nothing is impossible. We can create any changes we want in our life. Actually, we can create a whole world. Why not create our own planet, where every wish of ours instantly and effortlessly becomes a reality?

If you could create your own planet, what would it look like? What shape would it have? What climate? Would there be any inhabitants, and if so, how many? Would there be any people or other creatures? How long would the day be? And the night? Will there be nights and days at all?

How long would you want to stay there? Would you visit there every day, week, month? Would you move there if you could? What are some of your favourite aspects you have just invented? Could you incorporate any of them into your life now? Whatever comes to mind, explore it and write it down in detail. You're not committing to actually living on this planet—you're getting to know yourself, and you deserve to know yourself well.

CHAPTER 14

RELATIONSHIP
WITH POSSIBILITIES

EXPLORING THE IMPOSSIBLE

We have more possibilities available in each
moment than we realize.

– THICH NHAT HANH

Every now and then, all of us invent future scenarios—usually scary ones. We invent excuses that prevent us from doing what we love because "no one has ever done that," "that's impossible," "who do we think we are?" etc.

There's no harm in making excuses, except when we forget that we invented those limitations and start treating them as real. That's when we might become fixated on the imagined negative outcomes and refuse to see any other possibilities than the ones we had imagined. Thank God that life cannot be limited by our imagination.

Today, expand your imagination by playing with possibilities. Ask yourself a simple and powerful "what if" question. Follow the two words with as many possibilities as you can fathom. For example, you can ask, "What if I wrote two pages every morning? What if I ran five miles every day? What if I asked Anne out?" You get the idea. As an experiment, pretend not to care about answers at all. Allow yourself the freedom and the joy of exploring the impossible.

Start by writing as many "what if" questions as you can. Allow the questions to open up the possibilities. Feel the questions without rushing to respond to them. And if you feel the answers come, write them down as the second part of the exercise. The answers are less important than the feeling a true question can give. Asking questions requires courage. Sometimes we are not ready to ask them because we're not ready to hear the answers. If the answers feel too risky, you don't have to put them down on paper. Answers are separate from questions, so you can take it easy and focus only on the questions for now.

SHARING MY FATHER'S TRICK

*Our greatest weakness lies in giving up. The
most certain way to succeed is always to try
just one more time.*

– THOMAS A. EDISON

Many people have helped me by asking the right questions. My dad was the best. He rarely gave advice. Instead, he'd always question my belief in my limitations by asking, "Why not?" With this one question, he made me define the imagined obstacles, and after I was done building a case for my limitations, he'd reply with absolute faith, "I know you can do this, so what would it take for you to get this done?"

These days, whenever I think that I can't do something, I hear my dad's voice saying, "Why not?", and each "I can't" automatically becomes "What would it take for me to do this?" In the face of this question, obstacles usually fall away and become more like puzzles that need solving. "I can't write a book" becomes "What would it take for me to write the book that I've been wanting to write for years?" Every seeming obstacle gets rephrased as a possibility, and every intimidating goal transforms into an exciting adventure. What would it take to move across the world? To finish my dissertation? To write my book? To find a job? To feel the pain of losing my dad and to find the strength to carry on like he'd want me to? Thank you, Dad, for this amazing trick that I can now share with others.

Try my father's trick. Take three minutes to list all the things that seem impossible for now but that you would like to be able to do. The more you list, the more fun the next part of the exercise will be, but list at least ten. For example:

I can't sing.

I can't cook.

I can't travel around the world.

I can't be a good mother.

I can't finish school.

I can't find a good job.

I can't have a job that I love and spend a lot of time with my family.

I can't continue my current job.

Now rephrase every statement by starting with, "What would it take for me to …?" I'm always surprised by how some possibilities manifest in our life after we reframe our thoughts.

IMAGINING A PERFECT DAY

Trust in dreams, for in them is hidden the gate
to eternity.

– KHALIL GIBRAN

We have all dreamed of having a perfect life, where things make sense and our days are filled with meaning and purpose. Each of us has a different idea of what a perfect day looks like. Have you spent time fantasizing about it, journaling about it, drawing it, talking about it to a friend? Did you give it a concrete form, or is the idea of a perfect day still vague in your mind? Regardless of your answer, writing will give you a great platform for imagining and carefully selecting the elements of your very own perfect day.

Describe your perfect day. Do not think about any restrictions—feel the freedom of this exercise. In your imagination, you are not restricted by time, money, or your geographical location. You can be anywhere, even in a different galaxy if you'd like. Where are you? On a sunny beach or on top of a snowy mountain? What are you doing and not doing? Are you writing, playing, walking, creating, sharing, listening, or talking with someone? What do you see, hear, smell, and feel around you? Whom are you with or without? How would you start and finish your day? Do you wake up by the ocean and go running with your dog? Are you sipping tea on a patio wrapped in a blanket with your love? Watching the waves and listening to the tide? Freewrite for seven minutes.

WRITING THE BOOK
OF YOUR LIFE

Your emotional life is not written in cement
during childhood. You write each chapter as
you go along.

– HARRY STACK SULLIVAN

We are usually so immersed in the multitude of small details of our daily lives that it becomes very easy to lose track of the big picture. It's much easier to focus on the grocery list than think about your whole life developing in a certain direction. If you were an outsider looking at your life as a whole, what main story would you see developing? How does the big story of your life go? What are some pivotal moments that define who you are? Who would be the main characters in your story? Are you the main character in your own life?

238

Imagine that your life is a book. A very small book of only five small chapters and a brief one-sentence introduction. How would it go? What would be the title, and what illustrations or photographs would symbolize each stage in your life?

What would the intro say in one sentence? What is the first thing you would like to share with the world before you reveal the rest of the book? What is important for your reader to know right away? Don't bother with something too general, as people might choose not to continue reading.

Write in the third person as if you are simply watching the story of your life without participating. What would the first chapter be? Is there an image you would like to use? What are the five chapters and their order? What is the final chapter? How does the book end?

Are there any parts in your book that you would like to rewrite? Would you leave some pages blank? Why are they blank? Play with this idea through freewriting for seven minutes.

WRITING YOURSELF FREE

Words outlive people, institutions, civilizations.
Words spur images, associations, memories,
inspirations and synapse pulsations. Words
send off physical resonations of thought
into the nethersphere. Words hurt, soothe,
inspire, demean, demand, incite, pacify, teach,
romance, pervert, unite, divide. Words be
powerful.

– INGA MUSCIO

Often when we're looking at someone, we're reminded of someone else. Or we might be looking at something, and our mind takes us somewhere else via free association. The colour of someone's blouse may remind you of a medallion your mom gave you, and the whole time you are listening to this person, you are not really there. You are off on a trail of memories, having tea with your mom in your favourite spot at the kitchen table.

Free association happens spontaneously without our directed attention. Thoughts and images start spinning rapidly out of control and into complex and intricate webs. Words do the same. They can trigger a trail of memories, impressions, images, and feelings. They can inspire other words. We can play with words and harness the power of free association to get some unexpected answers.

Take a moment to go through your recent texts or emails and wait for a word or a short phrase to jump out at you. Write it down in the middle of a blank page. This central word or phrase doesn't have to be long or very significant. You can write down "I" or "but" if it speaks to you in the moment. The only requirement is that it genuinely speaks to you. You don't need to know why. In fact, it's best if you don't know why and instead allow yourself to discover new meanings through this game.

In the space around the central word, write down any other words that you associate with it. For one or two minutes, write down absolutely anything that comes to mind—especially, if it's strange, awkward, or surprising. You can write down as many other words as you want. After you've finished, freewrite about all the interesting meanings and associations you discover. You can start with, "What's most surprising is …" and write nonstop for seven minutes. You can make it even more fun and write a poem using as many words on the page as possible.

WRITING TO DISCOVER
POSSIBILITIES

The journey of a thousand miles begins with
one step.

– LAO TZU

Writing can be that first step. Regardless of what is happening right now, something else is always possible. By definition, possibilities are potential reality. They are limitless. Some of the best things in life happen when our realistic plans fall through and a beautiful surprise falls right into our lap, when we least expect it. Writing to find possibilities encourages us to go beyond our comfort zone, beyond what's familiar or realistic. It allows us to stretch our imagination muscles and start dreaming about possibilities.

Begin by writing down three possible scenarios for this evening. They can range from likely to most unlikely. Your favourite baseball star lost their phone and is asking to use yours to make a call. You don't have to worry about being realistic at all. Or, in another scenario, an attractive person might approach you in the street saying they have an extra ticket for tonight's show. After you list the three scenarios, freewrite about the one that spoke to you the most.

Now write down three different ways you could spend this year. Try not to focus on your current limitations. The intention of this exercise is to set your mind free so that you can observe where it takes you. You are not committing to taking a trip around the world just yet. You are only exploring a few possibilities. Freewrite for seven minutes about one of the scenarios you listed and reflect on what's important to you.

Wrap up your session by writing down three new careers you would like to explore in the future. They don't have to be realistic. You're just writing down three paths you are curious about in order to explore the scope of your interests. And just like before, freewrite about one path for seven minutes.

WRITING TO DREAM

*The true sign of intelligence is not knowledge
but imagination.*

– ALBERT EINSTEIN

When we were kids, we all dreamed of things that were both possible and impossible. Actually, back then, every dream seemed possible. What happened to those dreams? Is there anything that you used to dream about when you were a kid that got pushed out of your life because it was deemed unrealistic or impractical? Great news! In your writing, you don't have to be practical or realistic. Be unrealistic. Be impractical. Be idealistic and wild, and revisit some of your childhood dreams. It doesn't mean you must do anything about them. You are just meeting them in the space of this moment, writing about them and noticing what comes up.

Remember ten of your old dreams and list them. How does it feel to write about them? Has the way you feel about them changed? Are any of them still speaking to you in the same way they did when you were younger? Would you consider pursuing them, or are your new dreams more important to you right now? Maybe writing about your old dreams will help you discover a more complex and delicate balance between your old and new dreams. You can start with, "I used to dream about ..." and freewrite for seven minutes.

EXPLORING CERTAINTY

For my part I know nothing with any certainty, but the sight of the stars makes me dream.

– VINCENT VAN GOGH

Certainty is very attractive. Everyone seems to be searching for it. It promises security and permanence. We have a need to know things for sure. To understand fully. To feel like an expert. But is our certainty a true assessment, or is it just an illusion? What is our certainty based on, and why do we need it so much? Where does its importance stem from? What price are we willing to pay for certainty, and is there anything of value that uncertainty can offer? Often, we run away from uncertain parts of life because we find them uncomfortable. As an experiment, we could give uncertainty a try and learn from both sides of life.

First, explore what you are absolutely certain about at this moment. Write down, "What I know for sure is …" and fill the page with whatever comes to mind. Now give some space to what you don't know for sure. Finish the following sentences. After you're done, pick one of them and follow it wherever it takes you for the next seven minutes.

I am still not sure why …

I'm never quite sure about …

I still don't know …

I wonder …

I never know what to do when …

When I'm not sure what to do, I tend to …

I wish I knew what to say when …

I wish I knew what to do …

CHAPTER 15

RELATIONSHIP
WITH YOUR HEART
AND SOUL

WRITING TO FIND WISDOM

By three methods we may learn wisdom:
first, by reflection, which is noblest; second,
by imitation, which is easiest; and third by
experience, which is the bitterest.

– CONFUCIUS

We've all tried looking for wisdom outside of ourselves. It's human nature. We search for answers in books. We submit our hearts to other people's wisdom. That is until we discover how our own insights can come pouring through our heart and hand onto a blank page. Our own wisdom comes to answer our prayers and soothe our suffering. It feels simple and true, and it is very different from the confused state of mind we are in when we first start writing.

Writing can lead you to discover wisdom you didn't know you had. It usually comes as a surprise that deep inside, you already know which answer is rationally calculated and which one has heart in it. The latter comes with peace and liberates

250

you from needing to know if it is popular or even acceptable to others.

Deep down is that little voice we tend to ignore. It speaks its truth very quietly and doesn't care if we hear it right away or not. We are more than welcome to ignore it. It doesn't need anything. It doesn't repeat what it has to say. It doesn't insist on being right. It's just there. It doesn't need to rush or convince us. It will still be there when we see the truth, be it an hour or a hundred years later. It has no judgment because this voice is our truest self. It's our deepest wisdom that writing helps us to uncover.

Take a journey towards the deepest truths hidden inside your heart. Try to hear what your heart's wisdom is telling you. You can start by saying, "If I really listen, I can hear the little voice inside my heart say ..." and freewrite for seven minutes.

DRAFTING A LETTER
TO YOUR HEART

The best and most beautiful things in the
world cannot be seen or even touched—they
must be felt with the heart.

— HELEN KELLER

Think about your relationship with your heart. Do you have one? Are you friends? Do you listen to it, or do you give priority to the mind? How long has it been since you talked to your heart? Have you ever? Do you take it for long solitary walks? Do you pay attention to your dreams? Or do you write to your heart and get a response back? Do you hear your heart in meditation, prayer, or when you are playing music? How do you two communicate, and if you are not, how would you like to?

Write a letter to your heart expressing your deepest feelings and most difficult questions. Wait for a response to come and write it down, word for word. You can follow up with new questions, thoughts, or feelings and wait for another response. Cultivate this relationship with your heart. Have an ongoing dialogue with it. Ask things, listen for, and write down the responses. It doesn't have to be formal—the two of you have been closer than close from the beginning of time.

TENDING TO THE SOUL

Your soul knows the geography of your destiny. Your soul alone has the map of your future, therefore you can trust this indirect, oblique side of yourself. If you do, it will take you where you need to go, but more importantly it will teach you a kindness of rhythm in your journey.

– JOHN O'DONOHUE

Our soul talks to us every moment of our life, but we learn not to listen. It's calling to us quietly, telling us to slow down, be kind to ourselves and others, and to remember who we are. We usually tune her out and spend our days running around in circles going nowhere, listening to a myriad of other voices, except for the one that matters. We rarely stop to look at the big picture and listen to the truth of our soul, always speaking to us gently from the very centre of our being. Why are we in such a hurry? What are we running towards, and what are we running from? What is it that our soul is asking for? What is it that we're afraid to hear? And what would it take for us to pay attention to its voice and to listen?

Writing is listening. Writing gives you time to hear your soul and notice your feelings. It's in your power to hear and see. Writing invites you to trust your soul's guidance and have the courage to follow what you hear. Writing takes care of the soul and doesn't question its quirks. It doesn't judge, preach, or blame.

Writing gives space. It gives its full attention to the world, to life, to every cloud, leaf, and mushroom with full acceptance and love. Everything is included in this loving attention. Writing is tending to the soul. Listening to the truth of every single moment. Letting the moment sing, scream, dance, cry. Accepting it completely with an open heart and taking everything in with love.

Talk to your soul. Give her a comfy chair and invite her to talk to you. Ask her what she needs and what she has been denied lately. Ask her what she's been dreaming of and what would make her happier. Ask her to tell you anything she needs you to hear. Promise to listen without judging what she says or your reactions. Get a blank sheet of paper and start listening. Write down everything she tells you without talking back or justifying. Make it a safe place for your soul to share. Let her speak and keep writing until you can sense silence and harmony and feel your soul sing again. You can start with, "Dear soul, what do you need right now?"

BALANCING BETWEEN MEANING AND MEANINGLESSNESS

When you do things from your soul, you feel
a river moving in you, a joy.

— RUMI

Since we were first able to ponder life's big questions, each of us has been haunted by a search for meaning in our lives. Many books have been written on the subject, but so far, no one was able to find one universal meaning that would end the search for others. Meaning is elusive, impermanent, and personal. Things that are meaningful to one person may not be so meaningful to another. It doesn't mean that the search is not worth it. In fact, once you find what's meaningful to you, you can infinitely enrich every area of your life.

Right now, take some time to investigate which parts of your life are alive with meaning and full of soul, and which ones feel dead and are draining you.

Divide a blank page into two columns. In the first column, make a list of five things, activities, or people that add meaning to your life. What gives your life meaning? What are some meaningful relationships and activities you are involved in? You can list more than five, but do not stop until you list five. In the second column, list five things, activities, or relationships that appear to be meaningless. What or who drains your life of meaning and vitality?

Reflect on the two lists. How can you transfer some meaning from the first column to the second one that is currently empty of meaning? How can you imbue some of the apparently meaningless things, activities, or relationships with meaning? Explore these two questions by freewriting for seven minutes, paying attention to any discoveries or surprises.

CONNECTING
WITH YOUR SPIRIT

Trees are the earth's endless effort to speak to
the listening heaven.

– RABINDRANATH TAGORE

We are all connected to spirit, whether we are conscious of it or not. Even if it's not a conscious or intentional connection, most of us experienced moments when we knew that there was something larger than day-to-day living—when we felt that our connection to life is more mysterious than we understand.

How do you connect with your spirit? Does it happen spontaneously, or do you have a simple ritual facilitating this connection? Do you pray before bed, keep a gratitude journal, or take your soul for a daily solitary walk and feel into your spirit life? Do you call your favourite person on the weekend or hide in your favourite café with a good book? Do you paint, write poetry, write letters, garden, bake, or sit on a hill at sunset? What naturally connects you to your spirit? Did you lose your original umbilical cord? If you did, what came to replace your connection with your spirit? What became more important?

Write about the last time you felt a strong connection with your spirit. When was the last time your spirit felt like dancing? When did you feel so good that you wanted to hug every stranger and twirl them around until they began to laugh? Write about the time when you were happy for no reason at all other than feeling connected to your spirit and the spirit of life. You can start with, "Last time I felt like hugging the whole world was when ..." and continue for seven minutes.

If you could design a short daily ritual that would help you connect with your spirit, what would it be? It could be something very simple, like lighting a candle or saying thank you for the day you've been given. What would be the best time of the day to perform it? You can start with, "To cultivate a daily connection with my spirit, I could ..." and continue for seven minutes.

DISCOVERING
YOUR SPIRIT ANIMAL

Humans are amphibians—half spirit and half
animal. As spirits they belong to the eternal
world, but as animals they inhabit time.

– C. S. LEWIS

We have all experienced moments of feeling a strong unexplainable connection with the world around us. We suddenly resonate with the spirit of the water or connect with the soul of a mountain. We spontaneously identify with certain qualities that we sense in nature and want to cultivate them in ourselves. We see a beautiful slow flow of the river and want to move like water. We sense the stillness of a mountain and feel compelled to become still and grounded. We see a bird take flight and want to fly freely above our problems. We see a lion and want to be calm and courageous like him. Animals embody so many qualities that we can identify with.

If for just one day, you didn't have to be human and could turn into any animal, what animal would you choose and why? What animal do you identify with right now (you may change your mind in an hour) and why? What specific qualities speak to you, and what could you learn from this transformation? You don't have to be too serious—playful and curious would do. And you can always choose another animal mid-way through writing. Start with, "Right now, I feel like ..." and continue for seven minutes.

REFLECTING ON YOUR SPIRIT JOURNEY

My life is my message.

– MAHATMA GANDHI

In this book, you have already tried mapping your life journey, but today, you have a chance to focus specifically on your spirit journey. How has your spirit been lately? Each of us can feel where we are in the big scheme of things and what stage of life we are going through right now. If you focus, you can feel where your spirit is nudging you to go next.

Spirit doesn't need to use words—it speaks the language of images, symbols, and dreams. For example, at times, I feel like I'm sitting on a cloud and tasting every passing cloud, which is made of cotton candy. Different colours, different tastes, different experiences all floating towards me as I'm sitting on top of the world, happy to welcome anything that comes. Free and weightless, watching it all, and feeling like nothing can touch me.

Other times, I feel like my life is a runaway train. I'm chasing after it, but it's too late—it's already left the station. I'm carrying heavy suitcases as I'm trying to run after it. I could leave the luggage behind and run faster, maybe even jump onto the train. Or I could just let the train go, stop running, and rest right here and be fully content with it. Every metaphor and every dream offers a unique lesson from our spirit.

Feel into where your spirit is calling you to go next. What is it telling you to leave behind? What lessons is it asking you to learn right now? Metaphors and symbols could be effective tools in reflecting on your spiritual journey. Try to find at least one metaphor or a symbol for the most recent period that you are going through. Notice when this stage began. Was it when you started a new job, met the love of your life, got married, or had a child? Or was it when you lost your job, your home, your child, your partner, or your country?

Write down any insights you discover, no matter what your mind has to say about them. Your only job right now is to listen with an open heart. It's your own spirit talking to you. You can start with, "Lately, I've been feeling like …" and freewrite for seven minutes.

CHAPTER 16

RELATIONSHIP
WITH FAITH

WRITING A PRAYER

*Prayer is not asking. It is a longing of the
soul. It is daily admission of one's weakness.
It is better in prayer to have a heart without
words than words without a heart.*

– MAHATMA GANDHI

Prayers are powerful. They express our deepest thoughts, our most authentic questions, and our greatest fears that we would never admit to anyone but God or our journal in the darkness of the night. Prayers allow us to express our truth and speak to whomever we think is listening. And even if it's only you listening to your own prayers, at least someone is listening.

Writing down your prayers is good for the heart. It is already an act of faith because in order to write a prayer, you must believe that someone is listening and cares, be it God or life itself. Faith is worth cultivating, and writing prayers is a wonderful way to do it.

Don't worry if you have never written a prayer. Ask your heart to help you find the right words. Remain open and kind. Try not to expect an immediate answer to your prayer or your question. Answers may come mysteriously, and you may get a sign in the most surprising way. But you also have to remain open to the possibility that the answers may never come.

Take seven minutes and write one prayer from the list below. After you are done with the first one, you may continue writing another one. Spend at least seven minutes on each prayer.

Write a prayer for someone who used to be in your life. Express your wishes for them and silently send them your love.

Write a prayer for the world and send it love along with each of your wishes.

Write a prayer for the rest of today.

Write a prayer for a stranger who caught your attention recently.

Write a prayer for yourself as you are right now from your older self on the last day of your life.

WRITING TO MEET GOD

God is at home, it's we who have gone out for
a walk.

– MEISTER ECKHART

Writing is a mystical path. A safe one, too. If we follow it with courage, it will take us to God—to the end of our knowledge and to the beginning of mystery of our true nature. God is waiting at the end of each line. There is a settling in—a stillness—that occurs when you give yourself over to writing. But you must give yourself over completely. I'm not asking that you not be afraid. In fact, be afraid. Be very afraid and do it anyways.

Take this moment to write a letter to God, life, the universe. Express your gratitude and ask God some of your deepest questions that remain unanswered. Air all your grievances, yell at God in writing, complain about all the injustices in your life, admit your weaknesses and fears, ask for the strength to forgive yourself and everyone else in your life, empty yourself onto the page, unload all your worries and fears onto the page … then fall exhausted and rest in her lap. Feel her gentle hand on your head and the other one on your heart. There is room here for everything. And full acceptance is the eternal answer. Writing is a container for anything. Leave everything at God's feet and leave the page lighter so you can take a fuller breath.

ENCOUNTERING DARKNESS

Faith is the bird that feels the light when the
dawn is still dark.

– RABINDRANATH TAGORE

We have all encountered darkness. That overwhelming, crushing, and suffocating darkness. How we deal with it is very personal. Most of us run from it and distract ourselves for as long as possible. Few of us are brave enough to go right into the darkness and see what it's made of. Some of us just look up and notice the stars glow brighter in the dark.

Reactions happen fast. Do you even know what you do when darkness comes crushing into your world unannounced? Today, explore your relationship with darkness. Has it always been the same? What did it used to be like? Think about the last time you entered a dark place. What was your first reaction? How long did you stay in the dark place? What did you do to get out of it? What was your guiding star? What did you find outside of yourself to get yourself through the dark times? What inner strength have you found to move closer to the light? How has your relationship with darkness changed as a result of this last encounter? What are you less afraid of?

INVESTIGATING DOUBT

Doubt is a pain too lonely to know that faith
is his twin brother.

– KHALIL GIBRAN

Faith and doubt are two sides of the same coin, but acting on one or the other usually creates completely different outcomes. Having faith in ourselves allows us to reach for the stars and go after our dreams without much hesitation. Doubting ourselves stops us in our tracks and prevents us from taking a single tiny step towards what we would like to achieve or experience.

Doubting ourselves is rarely helpful. It requires splitting into two persons: one living their dreams without hesitation and the other one judging their experience as trustworthy or not. If we learned to trust our lived experience in the face of all the experts in the world and didn't waste any energy doubting its truth and value, we would have more energy available for responding to the present moment with faith.

A good place for investigating your doubts would be to start noticing which instances leave you feeling faithful and which ones cause you to lose hope. Start by listing five situations where you have faith in yourself and five more where you don't. Here are some examples of mine:

1. When I'm playing the piano, I trust my fingers to find the right keys eventually.
2. When I'm playing tennis, I trust my body to use muscle memory to find the best shot.
3. When I'm writing, I have faith in my ability to be patient with the process and remain kind to myself.
4. When I'm speaking with a class of students, I have faith that I will know what to say in the moment.
5. When I'm reading something challenging, I have faith that I can stick with it until I make sense of it.

And here are some examples where I don't:

1. When I'm playing a mixed doubles game with my tennis partner, I sometimes doubt my performance.
2. When I'm cooking, I sometimes doubt the process and my cooking skills.
3. When I'm teaching, I sometimes doubt my ability to communicate my vision clearly and precisely.
4. When I'm singing, I doubt my ability to hit the right note.

5. When I'm planning an event, I doubt my ability to think of all the details in advance.

After finishing both lists, reflect on what it feels like to have faith in yourself and to doubt yourself. What are some thoughts that run through your head when you doubt yourself? You can start by saying, "When I doubt myself, I feel …" or "When I have faith in myself, I feel …" and go on for seven minutes.

CONNECTING WITH YOUR PASSION

What you seek is seeking you.

– RUMI

Passion is like fire. It's a force that keeps us alive and keeps us moving when the going gets tough. If we have to do something we don't care about on a daily basis, it will soon become unbearable, and we will either break down or give it up. On the other hand, when we are doing something we love, we can lose track of time and feel fulfilled, even when we are exhausted. Even when we don't see the results right away, we don't mind because we feel connected to our calling in life. We feel as if we know a secret, that we were meant to be doing this. It's a secret between life and our own heart.

The same is true of writing. When we write about something we don't care about, our writing is lifeless and flat. Writing about our passion infuses our writing with the same joy and inspiration. We have to care, both in life and writing, if we want to harness the power of passion and inspiration. When we are in a rut and have lost connection with our dreams and purpose, we can remember them by writing about them intentionally.

Today, remember the time when something extraordinary happened in your life, something that connected you to your dreams and your life purpose in ways that strengthened your faith. Maybe you got admitted to a university of your dreams, or your first book was accepted by a publisher. Maybe you got a marriage proposal from the one you loved. Maybe you started your own business or got a great job. You felt that life was on your side and your faith was renewed. Write about what it felt like and what it meant to you in that moment. You can start with, "I remember very clearly …" and write nonstop for seven minutes.

QUESTIONING YOUR FAITH IN YOUR BELIEFS

The important thing is not to stop questioning.
Curiosity has its own reason for existing.

– ALBERT EINSTEIN

We all believe in something. Even when we say we don't believe in something, we believe in its opposite. We believe in ourselves, or we don't. We believe in freedom or in limitations. We believe that life is a friend or a foe. We believe in people's ability and good intentions, or we believe that we need to control everyone we encounter to prevent something bad from happening to us. We trust others, or we suspect them. We believe in God, or we don't. It might be helpful to identify some of our beliefs so we don't have to be surprised by some of them later.

Try to gather as many of your beliefs as possible so that you can take a good look and investigate your faith in them. Some of them might not be worthy of your faith. But see for yourself. Finish each one of the sentences below without much pre-meditation. Just write down the first thing that comes to mind, allowing yourself to playfully discover things. You can finish each sentence more than once and add new sentences to the list. Try to write honestly so that you can clearly see your relationship with your beliefs and identify those that no longer serve you:

I have faith in …

I believe the most important thing in life is …

I would never …

I should always …

I always seem to have enough …

I never seem to have enough …

Life has been …

Life will always …

My life has always been …

My life will never …

I will never have to …

I must always …

I have always …

I trust that life will always …

I believe that people are …

When it comes to God/the Universe, I always …

When it comes to God, I never …

When it comes to God, sometimes I …

CHAPTER 17

RELATIONSHIP WITH YOUR FEELINGS

UNDERSTANDING YOUR RELATIONSHIP WITH LOVE

Love is when he gives you a piece of your
soul, that you never knew was missing.

– TORQUATO TASSO

The word love is thrown around a lot without much thought or understanding. We use it with confidence, pretending that this short four-letter word can express the magnificence and the complexity of the feeling in our heart. Does love live in the space between two people, or in each heart? Does it exist outside of you, or is the whole universe made of it? Are you a channel for it? What is the source of love? The feeling of love is vaster than all concepts. And even though we can't know much about what it is, where it comes from and where it goes, we can still benefit from taking the time to ponder what this word means to us. Since it is a dynamic feeling, we could also learn a lot from reflecting on our changing relationship with love, our own love history.

You can start exploring your relationship with love anywhere you like, as you probably have a lot of personal questions about it that come from your unique life experience, but I've listed some questions that I found helpful. When you run out of your own questions, consider any of the questions below that speak to you, and freewrite about them for seven minutes.

Try to remember the moment you met love for the first time. Can you still remember where and how it happened? Remember your first teacher of love. What did you learn about love from your first relationship? Is that knowledge still valid, or have you unlearned it? How has your relationship with love changed over the years? What did it use to be? Did you once have love and then lost it? Where is it now? Is it in the past, or still hidden away in a secret chamber of your heart? What have you learned about yourself from being in love and from having your heart broken? What's the place of love in your life at this moment? Is there a place for it at all? When was the last time you felt overpowered by the feeling of love in your heart? When love knocked on your door, did you open the door or push it away? Have you learned to surrender your life to love, or have you learned to hold on harder to your need to be in control? You can start with, "My relationship with love has been ..." and go on for seven minutes.

WRITING TO FEEL

Thoughts are the shadows of our feelings—
always darker, emptier and simpler.

– FRIEDRICH NIETZSCHE

Every moment of our lives, we are feeling something. We can't get away from our feelings. We feel at peace one minute and get stressed the next. Joy is replaced by sadness in a split second. An infinite variety of feelings invade our heart each day. They can be confusing and intense. Sometimes we understand our feelings, and sometimes we don't. Sometimes we try to explain them away, and sometimes we feel overwhelmed by them. Some of us have learned to not feel at all. We think it's safer. Regardless of the circumstances, the feelings are inside of us—not outside of us—so we must look within and investigate.

Here are some questions that might be helpful in investigating our feelings and the stories connected to them. Start by calling up a situation that usually makes you feel overwhelmed, confused, or overpowered by your feelings. Freewrite about it using any of the questions below:

What am I feeling?

Why am I feeling this?

What triggered me?

What is this feeling made of?

What does it give me?

What does it prevent me from doing?

What story about myself does it support?

REVISITING YOUR
SCARY STORIES

Ultimately we know deeply that the other side
of every fear is freedom.

– MARILYN FERGUSON

All of us have been scared at one point or another. There are plenty of scary things in this world, like snakes or spiders, that can make us leap out of our seat and run for our life. But from time to time, we experience fears that are mere inventions of our mind and have no connection to reality. They are nothing but scary stories fed by our beliefs. And even though they are not real, when they sneak up on you, they can be extremely convincing and cause very real stress and anxiety. And because you're not aware of them, when they show up, you aren't ready to meet them. But the good news is that with the help of writing, you can get ready.

Today, take a few minutes to list your most persistent scary stories. Do not judge them as unreasonable. Allow them to be petty, childish, or insane. They are that by default anyways. No one else is going to read your list. What's really important at this point is that you collect as many of them as you can. Do not rush this stage because the more you collect, the better.

Sometimes, simply meeting the fear with open arms results in its dissolution. Listening to the fear, giving it space on the page, and responding to it with kindness can be all that the fear needs to feel heard and melt away. We all relax when we feel welcomed and heard. Why wouldn't our fears? For the next seven minutes, try responding to each one of the fears on your list without judging it. Enjoy this reflection and wait for responses to come naturally.

WRITING TO MEET YOUR DEEPEST FEAR

*Expose yourself to your deepest fear; after
that, fear has no power, and the fear of
freedom shrinks and vanishes. You are free.*

– JIM MORRISON

Now that you have given attention to the scary stories you tell yourself, you are ready to handle your deeper fears. You don't need to come up with a solution or a response to them. You don't need to wish them away. You can start by discovering them for now. Allow yourself to feel into the uncomfortable feelings of helplessness they produce in you. Stay with those feelings. Accept them. Feel them fully. If you honour the feelings by surrendering to them, they might reveal some secret gift. You might understand what you need and how to become free of such fears. Every fear holds a unique key to freedom—it's only here to nudge you through the door so you can reach it.

Right now, give space to one of your deepest fears and let it speak to you. Feel it, welcome it, listen to it, and write down whatever comes to mind. Set aside at least seven minutes and start with, "Sometimes I feel really scared that …" and give it time and attention.

WRITING ABOUT REGRET

Your pain is the breaking of the shell that
encloses your understanding.

– KHALIL GIBRAN

No one enjoys feeling regret. Not only does it seem to be a useless feeling, but it also often comes with its siblings—guilt and shame—and those are even less pleasant. So, we tend to see regret as a form of suffering and try to avoid it at all costs. But there is so much we can learn from it if we approach it as a friend rather than an enemy. We don't have to feel bad every time regret comes; we can take a breath and welcome the new lesson. Here's how.

List twenty regrets that you keep returning to. Write quickly, only for yourself and without details. You can use abbreviations to conceal names. Try to get more than twenty if possible. It's important that you get all of them out of your system and on paper so that you can detox your system and enjoy the possibility of taking a fresh look.

Now number the page from one to twenty again, and write down something good that manifested from each situation on your list of regrets. Remember all the interesting synchronicities, insights, changes in perspective, broken habits, and lessons that came out of each regret, and freewrite for seven minutes.

WRITING THROUGH ANGER

I would not look upon anger as something foreign to me that I have to fight ... I have to deal with my anger with care, with love, with tenderness, with nonviolence.

– THICH NHAT HANH

Anger gets a bad rep. It's one of many human emotions, but we have been conditioned to avoid it like the plague. We often attach shame to this already heavy feeling and try to avoid expressing it at all costs. So not only do we experience something traumatic that sparks the fire of anger, but we then shut the fire inside to make sure it doesn't get out, so the anger begins to burn us from within. Not only are we then hurting from the inside, but we are also shaming ourselves for feeling what we are feeling and, therefore, suffer the injuries in silence and shame. It's not very wise, but most of us have tried doing just that. Today we can try out a different approach to anger because writing offers us a much healthier option.

Start by simply acknowledging who or what makes you angry on a regular basis. List five people and five daily situations that are likely to make you feel angry. After listing them, identify a need of yours that did not get met. For example, if you get angry when people push you around on the subway, it might be your need for respect that does not get met. Take a few minutes to go down your list and identify one basic need that you felt wasn't met in that situation.

Now you can dig a bit deeper. Think back to a situation that made you really angry in the past but that didn't allow you, in the moment, to express your anger. It doesn't matter if it happened today, last week, or thirty years ago. What matters is that you notice that you are still holding a grudge. Freewrite about what happened. Allow yourself to connect with your anger—feel it fully, address the people involved in the situation, and explain how you felt. Write until you have expressed every shade of that emotion. Allow yourself to vomit everything onto the page until you feel relief. Try not to judge yourself as you are doing it. You are simply letting yourself connect with your true feelings and gather your thoughts and emotions from that unfinished situation. You are taking back your energy because you are no longer willing to bleed every time this situation pops into your head. You are not looking for understanding. You are writing to express and be heard.

Now sit back and close your eyes for a moment. Take a couple of deep breaths and write two responses: one from the person involved and one from life itself, offering you unlimited wisdom and compassion. Write until your perception of the situation changes from anger to feeling compassion towards the fear and suffering inherent in the human condition. Write until you feel love and empathy towards everyone involved in the situation, including you.

CULTIVATING GRATITUDE

Do not spoil what you have by desiring what you have not; remember that what you now have was once among the things you only hoped for.

– EPICURUS

ultivating gratitude doesn't take time. It doesn't require money or energy. All we need is a little practice noticing the blessings that we've already been given and giving attention to the fullness of our lives. Feeling gratitude is wonderful, but expressing it is even more powerful—especially in writing. Writing makes the feeling of gratitude more concrete and allows us to feel it longer. We can also go back and reread our entries whenever we need to refocus our attention on feeling gratitude and appreciation.

Today practice writing gratitude letters. They don't need to be long or complex. Be simple and spontaneous. The result they will produce will reflect the effort you put into writing them tenfold. Don't think too much before writing each letter. These prompts are just an invitation to experience the beauty of being in the field of gratitude. You can continue cultivating this feeling by keeping a gratitude journal and writing in it whenever you want to connect with this powerful feeling. Set the alarm for seven minutes and respond to each prompt until it's time to move on to the next one.

1. Write a love letter to your pet or to a pet you once had. Tell them how much they mean or meant to you. Express what you loved the most about them. Write their response as well.

2. Write a letter to your journal and articulate what it means to you to be able to express yourself fully and freely and feel heard. Just for fun, try not to plan what you will say and discover it by writing. Write down its response as well.

3. Write a letter to the part of yourself that you secretly hate. Find something to thank it for. For example, thank it for being patient with you and for never hating you back. Write its response.

4. Write a gratitude letter to your loved one and let them know how you feel about them. Write their response. No need to make this complicated. Use simple and direct language.

294

5. Write a letter to your chair, bed, or pillow. Remember those moments when you had nowhere else to turn and thank them for the comfort and support they gave you during those times. Write their response.

6. Write a letter to the person you miss most in this world, thanking them for making a difference in your life, for the gifts they've given you and the lessons you've learned from them. Write their response.

7. Finally, write a letter to love itself and thank it for everything it brought into your life. This is your chance to say anything and ask about anything you've been wondering about. Write down its response.

CULTIVATING POSITIVE EMOTIONS

It's not what you look at that matters, it's
what you see.

– HENRY DAVID THOREAU

For some reason, we tend to focus on what's not working well or what has gone wrong. We never need help noticing the negative things that happened to us and have no trouble wasting hours anxiously going over the various catastrophic scenarios of what could happen to us. We treasure these negative things like precious jewels and retell them a hundred times as if they are the only thing that happened that day. We might have had a great day, but a five-minute fight with our loved one could make us forget about anything positive that manifested, and the day becomes "ruined" in our imagination because all we remember is the fight. That's how skewed our perception is. Are we hopelessly hardwired to be negative, or can we cultivate our ability to notice good things in our lives, notice the beauty inside and outside of ourselves?

What if we treated all the good things that happen to us during the day with the same respect, attention, and reverence as we do all the little mishaps? What if we treasured them, and rushed home to tell our spouse, our friends, and our journal about all the good things that happened to us each day?

Today, take a tiny step towards cultivating positive emotions, and see how you feel at the end of the exercise. Answer the following questions and freewrite about one of them for seven minutes:

What inspires me?

What makes me happy?

What makes me laugh?

What gives me hope?

What interests me?

What am I grateful for today?

What makes me feel content?

What makes my heart sing?

CHAPTER 18

A HUNDRED THREE-
MINUTE SURPRISES

If you have reached this place in the book, you have done a lot of hard work and can now reward yourself with a little treat. You have done some deep searching, but there are times when you don't want to dig too deep. The next few pages won't require too much digging. The purpose of these prompts is to evoke a short spontaneous response that might surprise you. You can use them as a warm-up before a longer session or on their own.

Take at least three minutes to respond to each of the following prompts. The less you think about your answer, the more authentic your writing will be, and the more discoveries you will make.

1. The person who supports me the most is ...

2. The thing that distracts me the most is ...

3. What always gets me through hard times is ...

4. When things fall apart, I always seem to be able to ...

5. The three things that make it all worth it are ...

6. What keeps me going is ...

7. It's been too long since I treated myself to ...

8. Sometime this year, I wouldn't mind going back to ...

9. If I could add twenty years to my life, I would ...

10. I don't feel ready yet, but eventually, I'll have to face my feelings about ...

11. I wonder why I stopped ... I used to love it so much when I was younger.

12. My favourite moment after I get home is ...

13. My favourite moment during each week is ...

14. I've always had a strong reaction to ... I wonder if I'm avoiding it because ...

15. When I'm trying to avoid ... my favourite form of distraction is ...

16. If my heart could speak, it would tell me that ...

17. If I had my own secret room, I'd paint it ... I'd throw away ... and set it up in such a way that ...

18. If I could only save three things from a house fire, they would be ...

19. What I'm most happy about today is ...

20. The most memorable moment today was ...

21. Three things that went well today were ...

22. Three things that went really badly this week were ...

23. If I compare how I feel right now with some aspect of

weather, I would be ... (a February blizzard, an April shower, loud hail, a thunderstorm, a warm summer shower, a rainbow after the rain, a fog, etc.)

24. If I weren't so indecisive, I would make up my mind about ...

25. What has really been trying my patience is ...

26. If I could remove some unpleasant task from my daily routine, I would never again ...

27. Lately I've been curious about ...

28. If I could have one extra day between today and tomorrow, I'd ...

29. One way I can learn to trust my heart is by ...

30. One way I could surprise a stranger with an act of kindness tomorrow is by ...

31. One way I could surprise my partner (parents, child, friend, etc.) is by ...

32. For a while now, I've been feeling ready to ...

33. I would like to have more ... in my life

34. I would like to feel more ... in my life

35. Today I feel grateful for ...

36. If I am honest with myself, I need to stop ...

37. If I weren't afraid of failing, I would ...

38. If it wasn't so difficult, I would take up ...

39. Even after all this time, I'm still wondering if ...

40. If I could summon the courage, I'd ...

41. If I felt empowered, I would ...

42. Even though I don't feel ready yet, one day I will have to ...

43. A perfect gift to receive right now would be ...

44. A perfect gift to give (name) right now would be ...

45. If I won a million dollars today, the first person I would help would be ...

46. If today was my last day on Earth, the one thing I would do for sure is ...

47. If I could have an invisible friend, it would be ...

48. If I could only read one book in my entire life, I would choose ... because ...

49. If I could achieve one thing without any effort, I would like to ...

50. The person who helped me grow emotionally and spiritually this year is ...

51. One of my favourite nature spots is ...

52. If I could have a cartoon character on speed dial, it would be ... because ...

53. When I think of winter, I ... because ...

54. What I'm afraid to admit to myself is that I ...

55. When I feel into being gentle or tough, I notice …

56. When I think about light and darkness, the first image that comes to mind is …

57. When I think of being open and closed, the first thing I feel is …

58. If I could leave everything behind and move to any place where no one knows me, I'd move to …

59. The first time I felt free was …

60. Even though it is considered a taboo by many, I'm interested in …

61. When I feel helpless, I usually …

62. What would it take for me to fall in love with myself?

63. What would it take to forgive (name) and most importantly, myself, so I can move on?

64. What would it take to find joy in what I do until I can do what I'm passionate about?

65. When I think of their name, I feel …

66. The first thing that comes to mind when I think of summer is …

67. One of the most memorable and happy moments of my childhood was …

68. If I were given a free round-trip ticket to any place in the world that I could only use today and return tomorrow, I would go to … because …

69. What would make me happier right now is …

70. One thing I'm most proud of accomplishing today is ...

71. One thing I'm most proud of accomplishing in the last ten years is ...

72. If silence could speak right now, it would say ...

73. My fundamental relationship with life is ...

74. Being in love is ...

75. The point of having a heart is to ...

76. If you could be a tree, what would you look like? Draw a picture of yourself as a tree and freewrite about it.

77. If I could swap lives with any other person, I would choose to swap with ... because ...

78. If I could experience something in a dream that I'm not ready to experience in real life, I would choose to dream about ... because ...

79. If I could have a wild animal as a friend, I would choose to be friends with ... because ...

80. I can feel my heart open wide when ...

81. I can feel my heart shut down when ...

82. The three things I can't do without in my life are ... because ...

83. The three things I no longer need in my life are ... because ...

84. If I could be someone else for one day, I would love to be ... because ...

85. I never thought I could ... What helped me the most was ...

86. The three wishes I have for myself for this year are ...

87. If I could ask life one question, I would ask ...

88. Imagine that you met a mysterious being who told you a secret. What has it told you?

89. If I could invent a magic tool that could help someone, I would give it to ... because ...

90. One thing that I would love to start my day with is ... because ...

91. One way I could let go of my smallness and allow my heart to feel large and full is by ...

92. The three things I would never change about my life are ... because ...

93. Where does sadness come from?

94. Where does resilience come from?

95. Where do I come from?

96. I remember the first time I tried ... I felt ...

97. Twenty years from now, I hope to ...

98. I remember how good it felt to help ... because ...

99. I would like to express myself through ... because ...

100. What I have learned from writing about myself is ...

CHAPTER 19

MY FREEWRITING ABOUT MY RELATIONSHIP WITH ...

J ust some raw unfinished writings to inspire you to write freely. Notice how imperfect their form is. Notice how I digress and leave the prompt behind and follow my pen and my heart wherever they take me. Feel free to do the same. Playfully. Without a concern for the form.

MYSELF

All the mind-streams eventually flow into
the One ocean of Beingness. There are many
pathways for the mind; there are no paths for
the Heart, for the Heart is infinite and fills
everything.

– MOOJI

WRITING MYSELF WHOLE

Everything is here to turn us into love. I just want to know the truth. I'm so tired of being untrue. I want to be the truth that I am. Please, give me the clear seeing necessary to see and feel everything fully. Thank you.

What would help me feel whole is if I could go to Portugal and meditate with Mooji, sit in a cave, sit by the ocean and be still. Lapping waves would remind me of the impermanence of things, while the sky and the ocean would remind me of the great immovable spirit—free and unborn. Clouds moving, sand grains migrating, and waves rushing towards the shore and rolling back. Rushing, moving, but going nowhere. Just like us.

So many moves today, but silence and stillness underlie it all. Love is reflected in everything, but who has the time to notice? Everything is well and handled with great care by life itself, but who has the time to thank life?

WELCOMING ALL PARTS OF MYSELF

Here's a conversation I had with myself four weeks before getting married … again.

"Dear part of me that is afraid to get married again. I'm sorry that I have neglected you and pretended that you don't exist. I would like to listen to you and ask you: what are you afraid of?"

"I'm afraid of being mean, another failed marriage, betrayal, self-betrayal, uncertainty, revealing my dark side, making a mistake … I'm afraid that I'm not so sure."

"I hear and understand you. Thank you for sharing with me and for trusting me enough to share this."

"Getting married makes me feel scared, excited, and elated at the same time. No idea how it's going to go, and this is wonderful because I don't want to know. Following my heart

310

and my feet has served me well. I am supported and surrounded by light. As long as I'm letting it through, I'm carried and illuminated, but if I'm resisting, it's only an effort to change the illusion of me into a convincing reality.

Not to know—what freedom. Every moment turns into a discovery and a revelation. Every moment is here. Every moment is the only possible moment. Am I here to meet it, or am I running? From what and where to?"

OTHERS

Love is never lost. If not reciprocated, it will
flow back and soften and purify the heart.
– WASHINGTON IRVING

WRITING THROUGH A RELATIONSHIP CHALLENGE

Things don't make sense from here, but if I step inside his heart, I'm sure I could understand. I don't need to understand him in order to love him. He is welcome as he is, all of him, complete, incomplete, imperfectly perfect, perfectly imperfect. He doesn't need to change for me to love him. The sun can hide behind the stormy clouds, doesn't mean I'm going to forget that it's still there behind the clouds. So is my love for him. Empty. Loud. Honest. Still. Passionate. True. Forgotten.

HEROES

I admire Julia Cameron because she does what she preaches. She lets the voice of her intuition lead her through her choices. She writes without hiding. She writes as she is and allows others to do the same. She gives people freedom to be themselves by dropping perfectionism and sharing herself with others in all her imperfections. Her writing carries a mark of honesty and her soulful authentic voice. She did what no one else had done before. She followed her own vision and failed to notice that no one else was doing what she was doing. And now everyone is doing it. She shares her own writing and is not afraid to show her own process. I admire her because she is creative, original, and authentic. She is kind and doesn't pretend to know. She doesn't act like an expert, and meanwhile, she is the best expert on writing as a spiritual act. Writing and sharing it with others give my life meaning as well.

LIFE

I have just three things to teach: simplicity, patience, compassion. These three are your greatest treasures.

– LAO TZU

WRITING A DREAM LIFE

Here's how I would love my grandchildren to remember me when I'm long gone:

Grandma was kind and always allowed me to play with anything in her house. She allowed me to make my own decisions. Grandma always had a word of encouragement for everyone. She had a beautiful glowing presence and a permanent sparkle in her eye. Grandma was a safe person. She'd never ever rat you out or share your secrets with anyone. She was cool and had a great sense of humour. She knew how to have fun and let others have fun around her. She was never strict or mean, and never punished us. She was tender and soft like a cloud and always helped me out when I was going through a rough time. She'd help you secretly and wouldn't take credit for it. She was very wise and kind, and there was a lot of light and space around her.

WRITING TO FIND THE GIFTS

Here are some one my most precious gifts:
Big heart without borders
Abundance of love from family, friends, pets, loved ones
Trust in life
Thirst for wisdom
Appreciation of life

Love and appreciation of beauty, gratitude, acceptance. Gratitude is better than enlightenment. We accept what we are given and embrace who we are in the moment. Whatever the moment brings. The moment is perfect. Always. It comes from life. Life knows. And everything that comes from life is beautiful. It takes wisdom to see and accept it. I could use my sense of gratitude to notice the many details of life that usually go unnoticed or unappreciated. Life is here to shower us with gifts. We are here to watch and welcome all the gifts with open arms ... that is if we are wise. If we can notice with our heart. Thank you for this moment.

THE MOST IMPORTANT QUESTION

Today I feel grateful to be doing what I love. To have a job like this and a team like this. I am grateful for being able to connect with this group of amazing students, for each and every one of them. I am grateful for the clear way writing allows me to be honest and powerful. Writing opens a way to the heart and gives me heart. I am grateful for having a heart that can open so freely and spontaneously. I am grateful to be alive and sparkling in the light of God. I am grateful for life surprising me each day and bringing me gifts and treasures. I am grateful for many people around me and their kindness. Thank you for opening my heart to the possibilities of my life.

Thank you for the gifts I get from life. Life never asks for anything in return. I am so grateful to be here now, to take up this spot under the sun. Life flows towards me in such a beautiful way. Things appear and disappear like flowers and we swim through them like a river. Stillness in every moment.

A storm is a storm, and a heart is a heart. What's the big heart made of? It's made of a secret. It doesn't need to know why it loves. It is made of love. This is its nature.

WRITING INTO THE MYSTERY OF LIFE

Trusting life takes no effort. Why do I become so effortful and stressed at times? Why am I pushing the river? I suppose there's a place for that too. Allowing, accepting, resisting, and

316

rejecting. I'm only human, and there's nothing wrong with this dance of opposites.

Who is here to move and ask all these questions? Who is here at all times? In everyone and everything. Who is here to hear, and who is speaking from the silence? Whose hand is writing this? Feels like drowning—water and bliss, and no control either. Amazement, gratitude, and disbelief, acceptance, vulnerability, and complete openness. Complete lostness too.

I had my heart broken a thousand times, and yet it is still full and complete, even as it is going to pieces. Falling apart cannot be done by a ghost. I am not a ghost. This page wouldn't lie to me.

I'm eternally in awe of all this show. What a mystery. There is no point in even pretending to understand. Why? What would it give me that I don't already have if I pretended to understand? Space in my heart cannot be taken away by anyone. It can only be given away … freely. Freedom … it feels spacious and restful in this heart. I have landed into myself. Thank you for this revelation and for the safe landing.

NATURE

Beauty is eternity gazing at itself in a mirror.

– KHALIL GIBRAN

LEARNING TO WRITE FROM WATER

The water is moving freely and letting the light in and through, so that I almost can't see the water—just the light and the movement. The rhythm of water, so peaceful, so soothing, and so calm. Like the natural rhythm of life. It's here to support us and to teach us peace.

It doesn't mind other rhythms around it. It doesn't mind the noisiness all around. It's beautiful in its silence and peaceful in its beauty. At peace with the world, at peace with life. Everything has a place. Nothing is resisted. I'm often blind to all this beauty around me. It's transparent like water. Humility is its nature and a guarantee of concealment. The hidden nature of all the mysteries of the universe. The sacred heart of life.

Its secrets are not to be revealed to everyone, not until they are respected and revered, and never ever understood.

What a beautiful pause in my day, a perfect moment to come here to the water, get still, and listen to life. Clarity of perception is such a gift. When the mind is clear and transparent, just like Lake Devo in front of me right now, it doesn't obstruct reality with its murky perceptions. It's clear and peaceful.

Sometimes it even glistens with sparks of insight or inspiration. Seems like the clearer the mind, the more capable it is of perceiving the beauty and mystery of life, and reflecting it back to itself. Unknown, hidden places where only the brave ones go. Inside and outside.

The moments of clarity and of letting go are so rare and precious. The unimaginable weaving of possibilities in one moment. The very texture of life is uncanny. The orchestration of it all is so improbable. Life is here to surprise us if we let it. If we just let it. If we only let it be what it is. We try so hard to fit the majestic nature of life into what we know. What do we get out of doing this? A false sense of security perhaps? But we can only fool ourselves for so long. Eventually, the truth shines through in all its beauty.

We're all reflections of each other, of our true self, of life that forgot itself in each human form as a dance, a performance, an experience, a memory. We identify with the wrapper instead of the most delicious chocolate centre. Meanwhile, we are all sparks of the same divine light. We all know the secret, and the secret knows each and every one of us personally. There's so much love here that sometimes, it's impossible to let it all in. I'm afraid my heart may burst from accepting all this love. Underserved. Given freely.

We are born into endless gifts. We are all granted this incredible gift of life. Not based on merit. It's the nature of life to give and to rejoice in its own being. Just life playing with life and enjoying the game. Water moves and sparkles for no reason. It lets the light in because it can. And why not? The water is not concerned with what the light goes through. The content is irrelevant. It's all lit up and set on fire. The free fire of love. Throw everything in it. Let it take everything and spare nothing so the truth of our own transparency can be revealed by love.

GIVING MY TROUBLES TO THE RIVER

Water returns me to myself
Whispering gently the secrets it holds
Showing me that softness is stronger than armour
Made of illusions and fears
Captivated, I sit here for hours
Slowly, gently, water turns me into itself
Dissolving the secrets I thought I could keep
The wind sweeps my hair to the side
And whispers "love" into my ear
The heart wakes up and flings its doors wide open
Exposing its well-hidden wounds to the gentle sunlight

For the first time I breathe

Through my skin, through my hair

My lips are wet with kisses

I feel you near

The whole world is closer than before

So close I feel it under my skin

Inside my heart, embraced and warm

No walls

No armour

No mistakes

No missteps

No worries

No tomorrow

Now ...

Water keeps all my secrets

Returns them to me when I forget myself

Gently one by one, no time, no expectations

Just stillness speaking to itself

CLIMBING MY SECRET MOUNTAIN

Some mountains are not climbable. They remain unconquered for a reason. Giving up expectations of myself and others is my own personal mountain that I want to climb. Remaining with what is, being present right here right now is my mountain—seeing that everything is here for me. I want to be able to see clearly through all my stories. When they come to the surface, I want to recognize them and see through them. I want my heart to be guiding my body and mind. This is my internal mountain that remains unconquered. For now.

WRITING WITH THE RAIN

The truth is always here. Trying so hard not to know, or pretend that we don't already know. What is important right now? Rhythm. Health. Wellbeing. Honesty. Openness. Looking up. Looking in. Spaciousness. Awareness of everything that's going on through my system. Peace. Truth. Love. Spaciousness. Stillness. Centeredness. Groundedness. It's always here.

MY WORLD

Be content with what you have; rejoice in the way things are. When you realize there is nothing lacking, the whole world belongs to you.

– LAO TZU

LEARNING FROM THE STREETS

All the streets that I loved had an unobstructed view of the horizon and a canopy of trees. No obstacles, just the road ahead and a safe cover of green above, blue sky and sunshine finding their way through the foliage. Space around, space ahead, space above and a sense of firm ground underneath. Feeling safe and carefree.

Open space has always called to me. I seek it out in the concrete jungle of downtown Toronto. Right now, as I look outside my window at Elm street, my view is obstructed by tall grey buildings, blinding billboards, streetlights, huge parking signs, and traffic lights. They cut me off from the sky. The sound of heavy downtown traffic is deafening. The trees are non-existent. The sky is hidden by the concrete walls of the buildings. The light is hidden by greyness. No colour anywhere. Almost everyone is wearing black or grey.

And the trees. Oh, the trees. They look like they are fighting for their lives, tucked away in the dark narrow places between buildings. They strike me as thirsty and unwell, trying to get a little bit of vitality and water out of the tiny piece of ground they are allowed to drink from—not more than nine square feet. The rest is a grey, concrete canyon, canyon dwellers dressed in black merely passing them by. They don't notice that the trees are unwell. They don't notice that their own wellbeing is not supported by the streets or the city. The oppression of greyness is settling in. Before I wrote about this, I had no idea how important space, light, and colour were to me. Thank you, Elm street, for showing me.

BUILDING A TREASURE CHEST

Today, my treasures are hope, faith, appreciation, and an open heart. Being at peace and having a heart that sees the good in people and appreciates each moment. These are priceless to me. If I look inside right now, I feel relieved that my mom and sister are safe. I am hopeful. I dream of peace in my heart and in my country. I dream of peace for everyone in the world who is trapped in a war zone, or whose loved ones are. My heart is open and grateful. I am feeling blessed by so much. So many contradictory feelings are fighting with each other, but there is space for all of them. I love, and everything is welcome. Nothing is out of place because life has put it there, and I trust life much more than I trust myself.

So many thoughts, feelings, and dreams come to visit the emptiness that is all encompassing. So many strange visitors. Judgments come; I notice them, and I don't mind them coming. They are welcome to come and go as they please. Nothing has power unless I give it power. Life supports or doesn't support some actions or developments, and we're just here to be here. No agenda, but there's appreciation if we are lucky. I'm feeling so rich with appreciation for the wondrous gifts of life.

PAIN

Perhaps everything terrible is in its deepest being something helpless that wants help from us.

– RAINER MARIA RILKE

WRITING TO HEAL

Today I feel so raw and vulnerable. I'm not sure this is my pain, but I am not afraid to feel it. I am providing the light and the space for the darkness to burn out all the way, and turn into light and space again. Everything wants to return to its wisdom, and we are just luminous spots in the universe, and I am kind to myself and my pain, and everyone's pain too. Things are here to remind me who I am. I don't know how the moment will flow, but I don't need to know. I am freedom and space … and whatever comes just comes.

WRITING TO FIND REST

When I think of rest, I feel like I'm home. Things lose the dimension of time. They slow down and appear different. They feel more spacious and true, and I feel more clear and at peace. Peace is the underlying truth of all things. It's the dimension I remember well from childhood. Things have become a bit busier, but maybe because I'm not fully here to engage with what is here. I am at peace with myself. Nothing can touch me, I am aware of things coming and going, and I am peace that gives shelter to all of them. I am just here. Peace.

WRITING TO VENT

The weather is terrible
He never listens to me.
I live so far away from my family.
When is the war going to end?
When am I finally going to get fit?
Is the writing ever going to get easier?
Getting up in the morning is so hard.
Why do we have to go to work every day?

Responding to a few items from my venting list in a more balanced way:

The weather is terrible.

It's thirteen degrees. I still remember when it was minus thirty (just recently), and I thought anything above zero would be amazing. "It's sunny and a little fresh" might be a more accurate description.

When is the war going to end?

The war is making my heart larger and softer. I am more compassionate to other people's pain and have more appreciation for regular life, in which I don't have to hide from explosions in a freezing bomb shelter mid-February. I don't have to leave my home behind just so that I can save my child from artillery shells. My family and friends had to do just that and are still living as refugees for over five years now.

Getting up in the morning is so hard.

Being alive and having to get up is infinitely better than being dead and not being able to get up. Being alive and having to deal with all my daily problems is still better than not being alive. Work is just an opportunity to share our gifts with the world and contribute to the lives and wellbeing of others.

RHYTHMS OF LIFE

Happiness is not a matter of intensity but of
balance, order, rhythm and harmony.

– THOMAS MERTON

DESIGNING A MORNING RITUAL

I f I had two extra hours every morning, the first thing I'd do is open the windows and listen to the birds singing outside. I'd go for a quiet walk by the water and meditate on every step. I'd take the world in. Whatever comes up during that long walk, I'd attend to. I'd get the body moving and find some quiet place to sit down, have coffee, and write in my journal. I'd reflect on three things I feel grateful for and write a prayer for the day. I'd thank life for giving me another day, and I would look at my whys for the day and for the year and prioritize. I'd come home and make tea for my husband and cuddle next to him to gently wake him up. We would do some yoga and meditate together, and then burn sage to clear the space. I'd celebrate and welcome the miracle of the new day and remember that it's been granted to me. I didn't do anything to deserve it. It's a gift.

RHYTHMS OF THE WEEK

Being right here in the moment is my favourite time of the week. I am here fully, sharing my passion with others. I am free, and I am transparent. I don't know where this has come from, but this is a place for me, right here right now. I am here by the grace of God. This day has been granted and is running ahead of me. I am simply following. Just as I follow my writing. It takes me places that have their own light. I don't fear their light or their darkness. I know there's going to be something scary on the way. I'm ready for it.

TIME

Rest is not idleness, and to lie sometimes
on the grass under trees on a summer's day,
listening to the murmur of the water, or
watching the clouds float across the sky, is by
no means a waste of time.

– JOHN LUBBOCK

TIME TRAVELLING

Here's a letter I wrote to my 90-year-old self:

Dear Nata,

I hope you've learned to welcome the fear and do it anyways. I hope you've learned to love and not want anything in return. I hope you've mastered the art of freedom and have nothing but gratitude for every day that's given. I hope you've learned to spend each day with a joyful and open heart and have learned the difference between living from your head and living from your heart. The moment you connect with others is a true moment. There are no boundaries between us—we're all seeking freedom from ourselves. You're living your truth, and this is all that you can do. The rest is unknown and doesn't need to be worried about. Stay with your heart and live from it. This is the only thing that can bring peace.

REPACKING MY SUITCASE

I'd like to pack chocolate, Richard, my spirit—actually, I can't pack my spirit. It will be carrying me places. I'd pack some courage, mystery, and the beach. I'd also pack a lot of empty space for whatever life brings next. I'd unpack my cowardice and self-betrayal, apparent in those moments when I don't stay true to myself and act out of fear. I'd love to unpack fear, but I can't unpack it—it will come for sure. But I'll be ready for it. I'd unpack my ex. No particular reason. I just would.

I'd also unpack my worries. I'm used to carrying them around, but I don't know why I've been doing that. They don't serve me at all. I'd also unpack my alarm clock. For sure. I'd also like to unpack doubt, perfectionism, and heaviness. In fact, I'd love to unpack myself. Wouldn't that be the lightest trip ever! I'd love to unpack my desire to control everything around me. No suitcases necessary, I'm free. I'd pack some wings instead.

WRITE NOW

Using the same prompt on two different days:

In this moment, I'm feeling the beginning. Who knows what happens in the next few minutes. How does it feel to be me? I feel confused and happy. It's a great combination. Better than clear and stuck. I feel free to fill up the page with my thoughts. My thoughts and feelings matter. I notice how writing affects me, clears me, and makes me transparent.

Right now I feel like a tightrope walker, balancing between pain and wellness. What do I feel? The present moment only. I feel like I'm in the boat with spirit, being carried. I feel happy and alive. I feel alive. I'm free to have meaning or to have none. I'm free to not know what's happening. I'm free to simply feel. I'm empty. I am this moment.

This moment is full. This moment is ripe. The page is bursting. This moment is full with joy and truth and authentic power. This moment doesn't belong to anyone. It belongs to life. This moment stretches wide to embrace what is, just as it is, in all its fullness. This moment is a mystery and a celebration of life, a fresh breath, a true learning. This moment is filled with gratitude for this moment.

CHANGE

You have to grow from the inside out. None can teach you, none can make you spiritual. There is no other teacher but your own soul.

— SWAMI VIVEKANANDA

THE SHAPE OF TRANSITIONS

The same prompt on two different days:

Right now, I feel like a moth. Light, but prefer a cozy dark corner to a brightly lit stage. I feel in flight and yet ready to go to sleep. Ready to cocoon in the dark and hibernate for a while. My animal is seeking refuge and some quiet. It's been on stage for so long that it wants to rest. I want to hide away. I want to fly in the dark using only my intuition and my wings without needing anyone to see me, help me see, or navigate. Without needing any support on any place to land on. I am light and free. Darkness is as good as light.

Right now, I feel like a superhero who is shrinking. I'm inheriting new responsibilities and new roles. Some of them are unfamiliar and scary. I'm unsure. I'm melting and shrinking. I'm afraid of my own strength and my own light. Thank God life doesn't care and just keeps bringing on the challenges so that I have to dig deep to find my strength and power. I'm shrinking. I'm shrinking. My superhero is becoming a small cartoon drawn on a piece of paper. I don't believe its smallness though. And I don't believe its one-dimensionality. I feel the power of the heart within. It's like we all share this one amazing heart that's larger than life and can hold all of us.

I also feel like a wonderful snowflake that's floating in the air and melting from its own warmth. It's melting to lose its form and to merge with the underground water that knows all secrets but is hidden deep and seems invisible. Spirit is taking care of everything and will always do that. I can trust life to guide me and not to worry about things so much. Relax into peace. And just be the peace.

EXPLORING THE CHANGING

I used to sing and write my own songs, but for some reason I've stopped. I used to paint and post my art all around my room, but now I rarely do. I used to be my own boss and wander around the city for no particular reason, other than bring presence in my own life and my own world. I used to be me unabashedly. I used to compose my own music and play it for others, play the piano for others, play my guitar and sing my own songs, but now I don't own a musical instrument. I used to be free and be of the spirit, but now I'm more driven by the idea of responsibility.

I used to play hard all the time and was very disciplined at playing every day. I had to play every day, by my own rules as well. Rules have fallen down, and the lists of tasks never end, and I can do it all playfully. I used to be more curious about the world and know less and be much happier. I used to stage my own dances and be my own director, choreographer, dance coach, and a performer too. I used to be driven by what inspires me and move spontaneously and harmoniously with life.

EXPLORING THE UNCHANGING

Fall is here, the seasons are changing, and so am I ... apparently. The apparition is changing, but the reality is never moving. What freedom, and how much breathing space if I open up to this moment. I am here eternally—might as well enjoy this divine joke of ever-changing forms. It's hard to be convinced of its reality any longer.

ADVENTURE OR SECURITY

Dear Nata, I hope this time you fly, run, and be free. You spend most of your life going for the safe and secure option. This time, give yourself the gift of faith in yourself. It feels freeing to step into my own voice and be bold and have faith in my own wings, and not in the branch that only seems to provide support.

SPACE

Everybody needs beauty as well as bread,
places to play in and pray in, where nature
may heal and give strength to body and soul.

– JOHN MUIR

WRITING TO FIND HOME

Today I feel grateful that I have a home, a place where it's safe to be myself.

When I'm at home, I feel love in my heart, I feel joy and peace, I feel a sense of safety and complete acceptance. If I carry pain or worries during the day, I can bring them home and put them down by the door. I'm in my sanctuary.

Home is a connecting space. A secret garden where a soul can play and grow. A place where my heart softens and leaps into laughter. A home is a place where a soul can rest. It's safe, warm, and giggly. It's open. It welcomes and beckons us to return.

So many places I've called home. A home has a heart. A fire. A sacred fire of love that burns through everything else. We are all melted in it, so that we can sense our oneness and connection with life. Love is here. Home is where love is.

CREATING A SAFE PLACE

I feel a cool breeze on my face, and I am complete and fulfilled. So many voices are calling me, but here in my safe place, they are but echoes calling from far away. I've come to know them. They are here to stay, but their power over me is diminished each day.

My safe, healing place is always in my heart, and the journey is very, very quiet. I feel it takes no time to go from my head to my heart. Love can teach me. In each moment. My healing place is in acceptance of everything that's going on. Everything is welcome. Thank you for this moment. This moment is for this. Time doesn't really move. It stands still. We move. Life moves in a way that it does. It fills our hearts with life and our lungs with air. Things move at their own pace. Clear my mind, clear my heart, clear my light and move freely.

When I'm in my healing place, I'm always by the water. I hear the sound of lapping waves on the shore. It's calming, and I dream big. I feel my heart expand in all directions. It's in my own arms, and I don't leave myself to go to someone else for comfort. I am honest, strong, and empty. I am no one in particular, and life is just playing out through me. No obstacles. I'm in a safe world, and it supports me. Thank you for this discovery—I am feeling very grateful.

FREEDOM

Our deepest fear is not that we are inadequate.
Our deepest fear is that we are powerful
beyond measure. It is our light, not our
darkness, that most frightens us. We ask
ourselves, "Who am I to be brilliant, gorgeous,
talented, fabulous?" Actually, who are you
not to be? Your playing small doesn't serve the
world ... we are all meant to shine ... And as
we let our own light shine, we unconsciously
give other people permission to do the same ...

– MARIANNE WILLIAMSON

FREEDOM FROM MY MIND

Here are a few examples of me working through my unhelpful beliefs and replacing them with healthier and more compassionate ones:

I have so much to do in so little time.

I only have one thing to do right now. And at any point in time, it's always now.

I must not fail.

It's important that I fail sometimes. It's good for my wellbeing. I'm so used to winning that I am getting attached to that experience. Balance is better than one extreme. I could allow myself to fail once in a while just for the fun of experiencing it.

I can do everything for everyone right away on short notice.

I'm not superhuman. I'm just a person who has a limited amount of time in her day. I have to define what's important to me. I also have to take care of my body and not put it through so much stress.

I must accommodate and please everyone.

Who gave me this task? Why did I take it upon myself? Whom does it serve? Only my ego. I must stay true to myself and allow others to stay true to who they are.

The most important thing is to make everyone happy.

I've had such a good life. I've been so fortunate that when someone is disappointed or unhappy, it seems wrong and I take it upon myself to try to make everyone happy. I fail, of course. And in the process, I become disrespectful of my own heart and my own needs. I disrespect and devalue my goals. Things are equal—everyone is important. And so am I. The most important thing is to stay true to myself.

A SECRET ESCAPE

If at this moment, I had three hours to go anywhere in the world, I would definitely escape to a Caribbean beach. The healing colours of gold and blue, the gentle rhythm of the lapping waves, sand between my toes, sun on my skin—the perfect escape. I would cloud watch for hours, and then I'd ask the ocean, "What does it all mean?", and I would listen to the answer without pretending to understand this mystery. I would talk to the spirit of the earth, the sky, the water, and the mountains, and I would ask them: What do you know? Can I know it too? How can I eavesdrop on your secrets? Who gave them to you? How many minutes do I have left on this earth? Would you please teach me how to be wise?

WRITING TO GET UNSTUCK

What would it feel like to let go of every expectation? What would it take for me to do so? It might simply take letting go over knowing anything. Diving into the unknown with trust and self-compassion with all of my heart. Not ninety-nine percent but all of it—fully, completely. If I let go of expectations, it would be scary at first, as I would be letting go of control that I always thought I had. Things would continue unfolding, and judging them wouldn't be wrong, just not very wise. Wisdom is the ability to appreciate everything truly, with our whole heart.

ATTENTION

Everything has beauty, but not everyone sees it.

– CONFUCIUS

WRITING TO NOTICE

Here are twenty-five of my favourite things, in no particular order:

1. The first cup of coffee in the morning that my lovely husband brings to bed every morning
2. Talking to mom on the phone every day
3. Having such a loving family
4. Cooking a hearty meal and having friends or family over
5. Writing
6. Teaching
7. My freckles
8. Taking long walks each day
9. Sitting on the grass
10. My unwavering trust in life

11. My time in graduate school
12. Writing with others and sharing our work
13. Sitting on a shore and listening to the waves while writing in my journal
14. Fresh fruit
15. Chocolate
16. Five minutes on a swing before going to bed
17. Open green spaces with lots of sky
18. Pets—my own and other people's
19. Playing tennis
20. Laughing for no reason
21. Sitting in silence
22. Sitting by the window and looking at the rain
23. Walking or running in the rain
24. My community of yoginis, writers, and meditators
25. Practicing yoga

OPENLY WATCHING

Life doesn't stop for a moment or a day. It's moving me in its own direction. I have learned not to resist. I am moving with life. I am life moving. No concern for the form life takes today, just gratitude for life itself and the ability to be alive, to breathe, to watch, and to feel it all. Simple, empty, ringing silence watching it all openly and with gratitude. Grateful for the ability to be open and to be able to love. What a miracle—to be able to love.

RECONNECTING WITH PEACE

I feel most peaceful when I'm writing. It doesn't matter what is happening around me as I take the time to pay attention to what's happening inside. I own, notice, and cherish my interior space. I don't run out of thoughts, but my attention grows. My space inside feels cherished and nourished. Writing tells me secrets, and I discover them as I go along. Writing keeps me honest and makes me notice things. Thank you for my writing space. As I write, the heart sings, and I feel the wings growing on my back. Writing gives me freedom and joy. I am at peace. I am here. I am at peace with what's going on in the moment.

Writing is a life-long practice, and I want to be an apprentice of this practice. One can never be done with it. It shows the natural flow of things and a more compassionate pace. I feel grounded and true. It's important to be myself and accept all the parts, the good, the bad, and the ugly. No exceptions or resistance. I feel most peaceful when I'm in my heart and stay true and attuned to it. No expectations for others or myself. Just discovery. No pressures or stress. I invite stress to show itself so I can see it and it can be seen. Nothing can permeate this peace, this emptiness. I'm not sure what will happen next, and I am grateful.

MAGIC

*What lies behind us and what lies ahead of us
are tiny matters compared to what lives within us.*

– HENRY DAVID THOREAU

A MAGICAL INVENTION

If I could make any magical object, right now, I'd love to create a magical calendar. It would be able to stretch the days and weeks, and if I wanted to stay in the fall or the summer for a bit longer, I'd be able to stretch the calendar physically and add another week or month. I'd put all my tasks and appointments into it, and they'd magically get done, so all I'd have to do is plan properly. Once they are in my magical calendar, no work is required. So many things I'd be able to do then. So many jobs. I'd dream away and get things done on time. I'd share it with my husband so he can do his degree in less than four years and dream of other things. We'd still get to take it easy and watch the sunsets and sunrises, and dream about possibilities. We'd do simple things together and hold hands. Beautiful life.

POSSIBILITIES

'Tis the set of the sail that decides the goal,
and not the storm of life.

– ELLA WHEELER WILCOX

EXPLORING THE IMPOSSIBLE

What would happen if I wrote every day? Went for a solitary walk every day? Prayed, meditated, danced for no reason other than joy itself? I'd feel more free and fulfilled.

What would happen if I ran every day? I'd feel stronger and leaner.

What if I didn't have any more chocolate until my vacation? I'd either feel more proud of myself or way more irritated.

What if I wrote my book every day? I'd finish it before the end of summer.

What if I wrote what I'm grateful for at the end of every day? I'd be more aware of life's generosity.

What if I only did what inspires me and brings me joy? I'd be happier, lighter, and more spontaneous. I would trust life more and follow my heart with more ease.

What if I never criticized anyone or anything? I could use the energy wasted on negative thoughts and judgements to remain still and contemplate the mystery of life.

What if every morning I took thirty minutes to meditate? What if I didn't stop meditating throughout the day? I'd be at peace and more aware of my life, of my breath, of my natural rhythm, and I'd be kinder.

A PERFECT DAY

Every morning I wake up with the sun and listen to the silence, meet the new day, and listen to my own soul. I wake up by the ocean. I hear the waves and the birds outside my window. There's no one on the beach. My heart sings with the birds as I take a long walk on the beach. I connect telepathically with everyone who's dear to my heart. I send them love and check on them energetically. Love shows me what I'm feeling that day. Things go the way they always do, without my interference. I thank life for everything in my heart. My heart is as big as the world, and I move with the inner rhythm, focusing on the inner strength, inner space, inner peace, and inner understanding. I am feeling the present moment only. My heart is singing, and I feel the soothing rhythm of the waves. I'm not thinking about anything. I am feeling at peace, grounded and at rest. Thank you.

EXPLORING CERTAINTY

Creating space and letting go into not knowing—is there anything more beautiful? Loving the most amazing gifts life brings, always unexpected. I don't need to know anything. Life is so good to me. What is there to know anyways? Life gives. Love makes itself known. Life is beautiful. I am being breathed, walked, moved, and written in all possible ways. Where did all the questions go anyways? What remains is just the sweet sights and sounds of life. Love transmissions, heart-to-heart communications, so mysterious is this life. All questions are there to be distractions. I am here through everything, in every form, in every breath.

Never could I imagine that my life would go the way it went. Things are so amazing, even when they seem hard— it's only an appearance. What mystery is looking through these eyes? What is this eternal being doing here, in this body? This moment is a gift, and this one, and this one too. Beautiful mystery when I don't interfere with life and limit it with my imagined goals and intentions. Life is taking me for a ride. It's bumpy, it's beautiful, and the journey lies between the unknown and the unknown. From the unknown to the unknown we go. This beautiful aimless wandering is crucial for my wellbeing.

MY HEART AND SOUL

Since love grows within you, so beauty grows.
For love is the beauty of the soul.

– SAINT AUGUSTINE

WRITING TO FIND WISDOM

The heart starts purring and surrenders to the wisdom that comes pouring out and that I never thought I could access. First, confusion. Grievances, complaints, and righteous outrage of a victim. Word by word, line by line, page by page, that voice is getting more and more dull and distant, and another one appears from somewhere deep inside, a place I didn't know existed. A voice of a sage in a thirteen-year-old body. Where does it come from? Each and every one of us has this secret place to tap into. It's our birthright. Freedom, love, and writing can show us the secret door.

A LETTER TO MY HEART

Here's what came out one day when my heart and I were talking in my journal:

Some days just speed up without a warning. Feeling so many emotions at the same time. It's good to let everything be. Accept the love that is here. How are you, beloved? In love with the universe, as usual? This is good. Dear Nata, you've just turned thirty-nine. Life is beautifully unexpected and beautifully rich with all these tragic events and amazing support that you have. Water, sky, clouds have all been there to surround you and connect you to yourself. Nothing's ever been disconnected—you've dreamt it, little one. There's only love here, and nothing is missing.

Who are all these people?

They are all you in all shapes and forms. Formless you in all your incarnations, all feeling the same sense of I. How many lives have you lived? What do you need to feel complete? Why do you want to manage life or your emotions? Closer to the ground, in love with everything and everyone every single moment. You need do nothing. It's all happening by itself and doesn't need your help. Feeling helpful is just a trick you invented to not feel helpless.

Feel the core of helplessness, the not knowing and not understanding or needing to understand. Feel the love of the wind on your face, Nata. Don't miss the riches of life you're showered with. Don't miss the kisses of grace each moment of your life. What is it that you imagine stands in the way of your freedom? What illusions do you honour more than freedom and truth itself? What is here now? Right now? Attention, warmth, tenderness, and freedom. There's love embracing the whole universe, and one day is not better than the next for feeling the freedom that's inherent in your life. What is the form of your love?

Thank you for everything in my life. All the experiences, sounds, flavours, emotions, sights, and sensations. This is love constantly giving of itself. So generous. All these experiences that I'm trying to claim as mine belong to life. They're just passing through me, and I'm just watching and feeling it all. Nothing in particular matters, except the clear seeing that brings a sense of peace. My voice is silent, but it is clearest of all. The invisible is the most powerful part of life.

How do I know all this? Where did I learn this? In the heart of every human being. True knowledge is not learned or understood. It's felt. Every moment I know myself through my world. Everything points to who I am or who I am not. This is true knowledge. Rich and true and unspeakable. Love doesn't need any answers because it doesn't have any questions. Everything is everything, and we're not separate from it. How can we be? Love is taking me from moment to moment, and I trust its hand more than mine.

MEANING AND MEANINGLESSNESS

Meaningful:

Family

Kindness

Love

Spirituality

Trust in life

Meaningless:

Admin stuff

Daily minutia

Urgency

Falseness

Fear

Infusing the meaningless with meaning:

When I'm dealing with the daily minutia, I can focus on mindfulness and kindness as opposed to outcomes. I can let go of the outcomes and just be present and kind and open and accepting. Throughout the day, I can also be kind and compassionate to those who make decisions in the grip of contraction and fear, including myself. I can forgive falseness because it serves as a backdrop for genuineness and authenticity.

DISCOVERING MY SPIRIT ANIMAL

Today I feel like a butterfly, carefree and light. There's so much in this day that I feel like flying away. I feel like going higher and higher and looking up, not down. What's down is grey and insignificant; what's up is gorgeous and expansive and full of possibilities.

But I'm writing ... hmm ... do butterflies write? With their flight on air? I use my life, my flight as writing on air—invisible, yet indelible; unseen and hidden, yet very present and real. What's on my mind today? Oh wait, butterflies don't have a mind. I live as if I'm born today, and who knows when it's time to go out flying. So many things I pass by quickly. They don't stick, as I'm too fast. No stuckness, no hang ups—just flight and air. Empty head, empty heart—just beauty and freedom. Thank you for this revelation.

MY FEELINGS

Your task is not to seek for love, but merely to seek and find all the barriers within yourself that you have built against it.

– RUMI

WRITING TO FEEL

Every time I get overwhelmed, I sense something false and suspicious in this feeling. It doesn't feel natural, and it doesn't feel peaceful. I feel contracted and rigid. It doesn't feel like me. Life sparkles and shares its riches, but I am drowning in mental processing instead of enjoying the pure bliss of just being here and being alive and being able to feel it all.

Overwhelm consists of too many responsibilities I take on instead of feeling the moment fully. Who gave me such responsibilities? Life is so kind to me, to all of us, and it continuously sparkles if we let it.

The sense of overwhelm gives me a feeling of not being able to control things. When can I ever control them anyways? When I try to control things, it is always awkward and embarrassing. Accepting the messiness of what happens in the moment is great. It is the only option actually. Thank you for this. Life is amazing, and it keeps giving me opportunities every moment. I am learning about who I really am, and who we all are.

SCARY STORIES

Here are my responses to some of the scary stories I've collected:

I'm not good enough.

I am who I am in this moment, and this is good enough for now. I can always grow, but I accept myself as I am right now. Fully.

My boss, partner, or friends will not approve of me.

Do I approve of myself? Whose life is it? Whose opinion matters the most?

I will disappoint people I love.

Maybe ... maybe not. I can't know what they might feel, and I am not responsible for how they feel. I can never satisfy everyone. My decision is good by me, and the rest is out of my hands.

WRITING TO MEET MY DEEPEST FEAR

Sometimes, I feel afraid for my family. I'm afraid for their safety, their lives. I'm so far away and can't do anything about the war. Feeling completely helpless. Today, I feel so grateful that everyone is alive and well. My family and my closest friends had to flee their homes to escape the horror of war. They have been refugees for over five years, hoping all this time to be able to go home one day. I'm afraid for their lives. Never thought I would have to accept the fact that they might lose their lives in this stupid war. This is one of the hardest things I've had to accept.

So lovely to come here and just be with the sun and the water. The water is made of tears today. It's still very still and forgiving, and it's purifying my heart. My heart is awash in love and sadness at the same time. The paradox of being human. I'm happy to be alive and feeling my heart get softer and more open, more humble and more uncertain, more welcoming and more accepting with every bit of bad news I receive. The circles of light are radiating in the water. Light permeates everything. Water, sun, light, and air. The sound of water and of rustling leaves. My heart is at peace right now. Life brings teachers to me. I don't ever have to go looking. What is the meaning of war? I feel grateful to be asking this question, and I am grateful to be asked by life. Love is the greatest teacher. In the face of everything. In the face of war and its atrocities, the heart is calm and open. Love is pouring freely.

We stand on rocks and imagine they're stable and mean stability. I am grateful to know that there's no such thing as stability or security. There's only love. The heart grows and expands when I expect it to shut down, tighten, or harden. But it can't, because it's the heart. Love brings beings to peace and understanding. We are nothing but play of light and shadow, and even war and death are forms of love that we don't understand yet. Suppose it's a false need—to understand. Love just moves without understanding why. We are all moved by love.

Open heart leads to mystery. God playing as everyone. Every touch of sun on my cheek, every touch of wind. Freedom to be who I am. All the trials are welcome here. Nothing ever changes. Emptiness, purity, openness, and clarity draw people in. Like the beauty of this water. Life feels itself and feeds my spirit. It feeds itself. Until it's full. I feel grateful to know this secret.

NOTE FROM THE AUTHOR

Thank you for reading *7 Minutes to Freedom!*

Creating a connection with readers is what writing is all about for me. If you have any feedback or questions, you can email me directly at natalya@writingdissertationcoach.com I'd love to hear from you!

If you enjoyed the book, I'd appreciate a short review on Amazon.

If your writing could use a boost, download a FREE copy of *5 Easy Ways to Overcome Writer's Block and Start Writing Today* at www.writingdissertationcoach.com/free

And if you'd like to work together on your writing goals, book a free call with me.

I look forward to connecting with you! Thank you again for allowing me to share my writing with you. I appreciate every reader!

ABOUT THE AUTHOR

NATALYA ANDROSOVA is an award-winning writing and dissertation coach with over two decades of experience teaching writing.

Her passion is helping writers become more courageous, authentic, and kind to themselves. Through individual coaching, writing groups, and writing retreats, she has helped hundreds of writers to break through blocks and find inspiration, a more authentic voice, and a greater freedom in their writing and their life.

She lives in Toronto, Canada, and when she is not writing or meditating, she loves to play tennis, practice yoga, or sit by the water and cloud watch for hours.

Printed in Great Britain
by Amazon

74403594R00206